CREATING THE HEALTHY MARRIAGE YOU WANT

Stop Accusing & Start

Accepting One Another

BY PHILLIP KIEHL, LMFT
Copyright 2016

COPYRIGHT

DEDICATION

This book is dedicated to men and women I have met who have found the courage to participate in a healthy marriage.

I also dedicate this book to my lovely wife, Cynthia, who 16 years ago decided to go on a journey with me building a healthy marriage. We have come a long way honey, and I am happy we too have moved from accusations to acceptance. And I love you for this.

ACKNOWLEDGMENTS

I feel the need to begin by being vulnerable and acknowledge I am not a writer. Yes, I have two graduate degrees which demanded of me to write many term papers, but I never had a desire to write a book. When I was 40 years old pursuing a graduate degree, I had to take Greek. It was there I was exposed to not knowing English. I was humbled. I guess I snoozed through high school when I took English, as I had difficulty in this Greek class knowing the difference between a noun and a verb.

But as life unfolds, you can learn from your mistakes and weakness, and this book is an acknowledgement of this accomplishment. I am forever grateful to my lovely wife, Cynthia, who graded and edited my term papers back then and has been a constant help with my writing and speaking. Her editing of this book has pushed her patience in helping me with her red pen and glasses. I am thankful for her influence. Deep down, secretly, she always hoped I would write a book someday.

I also want to acknowledge two men who have shaped my life tremendously: Dr. Henry Cloud and Dr. John Townsend. Their speaking, writing, and seminars have helped shape me to who I am today as a therapist and person. I am also very grateful to my editor, Beth-Marie Miller, as her keen insights and suggestions have made this a better book.

Contents

Dedication   **3**

Acknowledgments   **5**

Introduction   **11**

Preface   **15**

PART ONE: What Is Healthy Versus Unhealthy?   **21**

Chapter 1: What Are the Traits of a Healthy
Versus an Unhealthy Marriage?   **23**

Chapter 2: What are the Traits Of Healthy
Versus Unhealthy Intention?   **29**

PART TWO: The Top Ten Differences   **35**

Chapter 3: Difference #1

Do You Want the Marriage To Be
All About You or All About Us?   **37**

    Unhealthy Intention: Focus on You   **38**

    Healthy Intention: Focus on Us   **42**

Chapter 4: Difference #2

Do You Want To Be Right Or Do You
Want To Pursue A Love Relationship?   **55**

    Unhealthy Intention: Focus on Being Right   **56**

    Healthy Intention: Focus on Being Loved   **61**

Chapter 5: Difference #3

Do You Want To Correct
Or Do You Want To Accept?   **67**

    Unhealthy Intention: Focus On Correcting   **68**

    Healthy Intention: Focus on Accepting   **73**

Pointing Out Unhealthy Behavior
with Loving Intention   **75**

Chapter 6: Difference #4

Do You Want To Criticize
Or Do You Want To Encourage?   **85**
Unhealthy Intention: Focus on Being Critical   **86**
Healthy Intention: Focus on Encouraging   **90**

Chapter 7: Difference #5

Do You Want To Be Resentful
Or Do You Want To Be Forgiving?   **99**
Unhealthy Intention: Focus on Resentment   **100**
Healthy Intention: Focus on Forgiveness   **106**

Chapter 8: Difference #6

Do You Want To Pursue Justice
Or Do You Want To Pursue Mercy?   **115**
Unhealthy Intention: Focus on Justice   **116**
Healthy Intentions: Focus on Mercy   **122**

Chapter 9: Difference #7

Do You Want To Avoid Conversation
Or Do You Want To Clarify Conversation?   **129**
Unhealthy Intention: Focus on
Avoiding Conversation   **130**
Healthy Intention: Focus on Clarifying   **137**

Chapter 10: Difference #8

Do You Want To Focus On Past Hurts
Or Present Hurts?   **145**
Unhealthy Intention: Focus on the Past   **146**
Healthy Intention: Focus on the Present   **150**

Chapter 11: Difference #9

Do You Want To Pursue Ideal Expectations Or
Do You Want To Pursue Realistic Expectations? **159**
Unhealthy Intention: Focus on
Ideal Expectations   **160**
Healthy Intention: Focus on
Realistic Expectations   **167**

Chapter 12: Difference #10
Do You Want to Pursue Control
Or Do You Want to Pursue Freedom?   175
    Unhealthy Intention: Focus on Control   176
    Healthy Intention: Focus on Freedom   181

PART THREE: KEYS TO IMPROVE YOUR MARRIAGE   191

Chapter 13: Keys To Improve Your Marriage   193
Chapter 14: Keys For Each Spouse
    Begin With Examining Yourself   195
    Own Your Pain   196
    Accountability Partners   197
    Declaration Page to Yourself   200
    Be a Tortoise and Not a Hare   202
Chapter 15: Keys for Both Spouses   205
    Admit We Have a Problem   206
Chapter 16: Summary   215
Notes   217
About the Author   219

INTRODUCTION

In today's world, spouses are finding it harder than ever to stay connected and remain married. Spouses have turned to the strategy of accusing each other, hoping this will fix the marriage. But after countless attempts to do this, each spouse feels hurt and lonely. Have you said recently to yourself, "Why do we blame one another so much? Why are we not happy and connected in comparison to other couples I know? Is there something wrong with me, you, or us?"

This book will challenge you to look at yourself in the mirror and determine whether you as an individual are healthy or you as a couple are healthy in the way we treat one another. You will assess by answering these questions: "What do I do to contribute to the health or unhealthiness of this marriage?" "Why do I accuse, or why does my spouse accuse me, and these accusations lead to hostility and hurt?" "What am I do doing or what are we doing that we cannot accept each other, but instead blame each other?"

Using the top ten differences, this book has been designed to help you evaluate your marriage in a concise manner by knowing what the traits are and patterns of a healthy marriage versus an unhealthy marriage. Stop the madness of accusing one another and learn how to accept one another. Acceptance does not mean ignoring serious problems such as cheating, drugs, alcoholism, pornography, or abusive patterns. But fixing one another's problems will never lead to accepting one another for better or for worse.

As a Licensed Marriage and Family Therapist, I know firsthand in my marriage of sixteen years how my wife and I have been challenged with these ten differences and have learned to stop accusing one another and accept one another. Trust me; I know this is not easy. But in my years of counseling couples, I have witnessed incredible results when spouses stop accusing one another and become healthy spouses for their marriage. As a result of learning these ten differences and applying this knowledge to your marriage, you will find that you are less lonely, less frustrated and angry, and have more resolution and a deeper understanding connection in your marriage.

I dare you to start moving from unhealthy to healthy patterns practicing these differences and becoming a happier person for a happy marriage. I promise you a healthy marriage is possible as you take the time to work and apply these principles to become two accepting spouses. My goal is to save your marriage from being another statistic of divorce like other marriages you know, and participate in making a positive difference in your marriage for the sake of connection with your spouse. So don't avoid, don't quit, and stop accusing immediately for the sake of your marriage. Do it for you and do it for each other and do it now!

So my invitation and challenge for you and the sake of your marriage is to take the stand and start reading this book, assessing the top ten differences between an unhealthy and a healthy marriage. Stop waiting for him or her to change, stop waiting for the stars to line up perfectly or for life to be fair. Take initiative and be a difference maker for your marriage. Set the example with your spouse so that other couples will start to compare their unhappy lonely marriages to yours and will want to know what the secret is, why your marriage is happy and connected. As you begin to implement this healthy behavior, others will begin to notice, and they will want to learn from you how you and your spouse became happy. You can then give a testimony to the hard work you have done creating the healthy marriage you and your spouse both want.

PREFACE

In general, spouses don't just wake up one day and decide, 'Hey, I want to be an unhealthy person, and my goal is to create an unhealthy marriage.' Hopefully each spouse does not make it a new year's resolution to be an unhealthy spouse. But the reality of life is that all of us, purposely or not, end up hurting one another, and these relationship hurts result in a pattern of creating unhealthy marriages and unhappy people. When two people have difficulty resolving relationship hurts, this will only lead to prolonging patterns of an unhealthy marriage.

You probably want to be healthy—many people today are focused on wanting to make healthy choices. Bookstores have been flooded with books on which foods to eat, which restaurants to choose, and how to maintain fitness. Overall our society seems to want to create healthy over unhealthy in all areas of life. I'm inviting you to create a healthy marriage.

In Part One I want to discuss two key qualities that make up or describe key differences between healthy and unhealthy marriages. The goal of this section is for each spouse to understand in general what it means to be healthy. What are the traits, habits, and descriptions of becoming healthy versus unhealthy? Over the years, research, observation, and experience in the field of marriage therapy have increased our understanding of what it takes to create a healthy marriage. When healthy relationship happens, then the fruit or the rewards are two people who are healthy, participating in building a healthy marriage.

I also discuss the important concept of intentions. Have you ever wondered where your spouse is coming from? What are they saying and why? When you understand the intention of the other person, maybe you can reduce the conflict between the two of you by understanding where that person is coming from. Healthy intentions lead to desiring and wanting a healthy marriage, whereas unhealthy intentions lead to spouses only focusing on themselves.

In Part Two I want to talk about the top ten differences between healthy and unhealthy intentions. My biggest fear is that you will use what you learn from this book as weapons or strategies to separate or divorce your spouse. That is not my intention. I am FOR spouses and FOR marriage, and we all need to understand that every marriage is made up of two broken people who will and do hurt one another. At the beginning of each of these differences, I have included a brief quiz for the means of examining your marriage. There is no score to compute for these questions. I also have included at the end of each of the differences some suggestions about what to do, to both improve and address that particular difference for your marriage.

The saying is true: hurting people hurt people. And who amongst us has never been hurt? It is easy for hurting spouses to quit working on themselves or the marriage, and then they get blindsided when one spouse wants to quit or has an affair, or pulls away and pursues other activities. A healthy marriage takes two people wanting to both pursue and intentionally engage in the process of creating a healthy marriage. When this happens, it is a set up for a marathon where both people want to finish their life with one another. Healthy spouses view the marriage as a marathon, unhealthy spouses view the marriage as a hundred yard dash.

In Part Three, I provide some keys and strategies you can do to improve your marriage. As a spouse reading this book, I provide some steps you can do to become a healthier spouse for your marriage. I also outline some steps and solutions for both spouses as they work on finding healthier ways to relate to each other. I know that change is difficult and can be one of the biggest hurdles for our lives. So be patient as you learn these strategies and don't quit, but really do recognize that healing is possible to build a marriage where two people are not accusing one another with unhealthy intentions and move to accepting one another with healthy intentions.

As you read this book, hopefully you will find yourself wanting to participate in a healthy marriage. I have always taken the stance that a happier life results from building healthy relationships. When you are loved and giving love, when you are trustworthy and building trusting relationships, overall your life goes more smoothly and is more fulfilling. When you are able to recognize how stress, conflict, and hurt from unhealthy patterns affect you and the marriage, then you will want to pursue and engage in healthier ways. A good and happy life is filled with love and trust from both spouses giving and receiving healthy accepting responses to and from each other.

In addition, this book is similar to a common theme today as people are focused on wanting to make healthy choices. In the area of eating and nutrition, books today give advice on which foods to eat, advice on eating this and not eating that, and suggestions on what healthy restaurants or eating places to choose. People today do want to learn to eat this and not eat that with the overall emphasis on wanting to eat healthier. In general, unhealthy marriages are focused on fixing their spouse's problems in their pursuit of arguing what he or she should be doing differently. Healthy marriages are focused on accepting one another and concerned with how 'we' together are participating and engaging in creating a healthy marriage.

So thanks for choosing this book to begin the journey of building a healthy marriage. A marriage does take work and time, but if you value a healthy marriage and are seeking ways to create it, I can promise you, it is possible and very rewarding. So use this book to evaluate your marriage, your spouse and yourself: affirm things you are already doing right, and discover how you can build a healthier marriage.

PART ONE

WHAT IS HEALTHY VERSUS UNHEALTHY?

CHAPTER 1

WHAT ARE THE TRAITS OF A HEALTHY VERSUS AN UNHEALTHY MARRIAGE?

What do you think of when describing what is a healthy or an unhealthy marriage? Maybe this is something that you don't think about, or maybe you are so used to being in an unhealthy marriage that you've forgotten what healthy looks like, and now your unhealthy marriage seems normal for you. Do you know what a healthy or unhealthy marriage is? Have you ever sat down and thought about the spouse in your life and considered: What are some of the healthy character traits of our marriage that bring intimacy and trust? What are some of the character traits that lead to conflict, doubt, fear, and mistrust for our marriage?

For example, when it comes to our eating habits, you may know the importance of looking over ingredients and checking out the numbers when it comes to fat content, calories, carbohydrates, and both salt and sugar intake. Today our society is a lot more educated and smart when it comes to checking out the numbers on food items at a restaurant or the numbers on the back of a package to determine if the numbers line up with what you would consider healthy or unhealthy. And this is good by taking responsibility for our health and seeking to become healthier. But what about your marriage? What ingredients make up a healthy marriage? For example, what if I were to ask of you to choose a recipe for lasagna? One recipe calls for cheese, tomato sauce, noodles, ground beef, and sausage. Another uses eggplant, spinach, and pesto instead of the meat. The third recipe includes high fructose corn syrup, heavy cream, and sugar.

What you prefer is your own individual choice and your own personal preference. However, what we eat affects our bodies, and some ingredients are healthier than others. All of us need to figure out what we want when it comes to healthy or unhealthy foods. The first two recipes both have healthy ingredients, but they will taste different and provide different nutrients. The third may make a tasty sauce, but if those ingredients become a pattern, there may be negative consequences.

So when it comes to marriage, you also need to think and choose what you want or don't want for your marriage. Healthy marriages don't all look exactly the same, but they have common ingredients. For example, do features and traits such as honesty, faithfulness, commitment, listening, love, acceptance and trust sound like they might be important traits and features for a healthy marriage? Are these traits and features something you would like and want to have to make up a healthy relationship?

Perhaps you would also think about unhealthy

25

WHAT ARE THE TRAITS OF A HEALTHY VERSUS AN UNHEALTHY MARRIAGE?

features of marriage. They might be the opposite of the traits I described above and could include lying, criticism, apathy, suspicion, and feeling trapped. Can you recognize the difference between what it is like to be with someone who you trust completely (healthy) and constantly feeling nervous or suspicious (unhealthy)? Far too often we falsely assume an unhealthy spouse will change over time, or even worse, spouses start to think they can change or fix the other person in order to be healthy.

Let's say you go to your favorite nursery or garden center and you buy a plant for your back porch. You look around at the nursery and you choose a plant that looks healthy, and you envision this plant at your house. The leaves, the flowers, the fruit, and the branches all look healthy, so you purchase it.

But now the challenge is to keep it healthy once you bring it home. In general, all plants need four main things to help them stay healthy: soil, light, water and pruning. Plants vary in the type of soil they need, and the amount of water, light and pruning it needs. Every now and then, you need to get the shears and cut away some branches that are not growing and not contributing to the healthiness of the plant. In the same way, even good marriages can use pruning now and then as the couple takes a look at themselves and their marriage to see what is missing, and what attitudes or behaviors have snuck in that they need to get rid of. A sign of a healthy plant is that it grows and it produces a flower or fruit. With the right combination of ingredients and care, your plant will continue to grow and produce fruit, giving you delight and pleasure.

In the same way, healthy marriages need four main things: love, respect, freedom, and trust. When these four things are missing, you will experience an unhealthy marriage. But when two people are in agreement viewing these four needs as a foundation for a healthy relationship, the relationship will grow, and it will produce fruit. Healthy marriages grow over time, and the fruit is intimacy, closeness, laughter, happy feelings, enjoying each other's company, and a sense of peace and security in knowing and feeling loved. Just like all plants need regular maintenance and attention to produce the benefits of flower or fruit, all healthy relationships need attention, investment, and regular maintenance to grow the fruit for both spouses to enjoy and experience.

So when you choose a favorite plant at your local nursery, your initial intentions are good, and your goal and desires are good. But over time, life gets busy, other things demand your attention, events you never planned happen, and soon your plant is starting not to look so good. Your plant starts to feel neglected—the soil has dried out, it's in a corner of the porch without much light, and you haven't had time to prune it. The leaves and branches are starting to droop, you had expected some type of flower or fruit, but nothing appears. Maybe you start to see some bugs or critters on the

27

WHAT ARE THE TRAITS OF A HEALTHY VERSUS AN UNHEALTHY MARRIAGE?

plant, and maybe the plant overall just looks sick due to lack of attention.

It works the same way in marriage. All spouses and healthy marriages need love, respect, freedom and trust. If jealousy, meanness, disrespect, control, mistrust, lying, cheating, or even simple neglect enter your marriage, you will not receive the benefits of what a healthy marriage will produce, but instead, you will feel insecure, accused, blamed, unhappy, worried, and a general sense the other person is just not that into you.

Healthy marriages take an investment of time and attention, consistently giving the right amount of ingredients, and looking for ways to experience the benefits and joys of this love relationship. Unhealthy marriages may have intentional unkindness, but they may also have less obvious problems like busyness leading to neglect, or the partners not really understanding or listening to each other.

So reflect upon your marriage and discern for yourself: Do you have a healthy or an unhealthy marriage? Or is it healthy in some ways and unhealthy in others? What healthy character traits do you want, and which unhealthy character traits do you want to avoid or get rid of in your marriage? In this next chapter, I want to inform you about the importance of understanding intentions in your marriage. As you read, find yourself answering this question: Am I for this marriage, and is my spouse for this marriage?

CHAPTER 2

WHAT ARE THE TRAITS OF HEALTHY VERSUS UNHEALTHY INTENTION?

Another important feature to consider when looking at the difference between healthy and unhealthy marriages is the topic of intention. How would you define intention? What words or examples might you think of when it comes to using this word in the context of a healthy or unhealthy marriage? Intention as it applies to marriage is very important because often one spouse may not fully understand or find meaning in what the other person is saying or doing. If you know and understand where the other person is coming from and what their aim or goal is (their intention), then you might be more understanding of why they do certain things.

In general, intention is about the end goal or the purpose for why someone is acting or saying something. So if a spouse has a good intention this coming Valentine's Day to bring home candy, jewelry, or flowers because he wants to express acts of love to his spouse, hopefully in a healthy relationship, the receiving spouse has a good understanding of that person's intention. He wants to express his love for her through these gifts. So healthy intention communicates a goal to the other person, so that the receiving person has no doubt or confusion of what his or her clear intentions are. There is less use of these words: "I don't understand why or what you are doing." Each person is singing from the same song page. Sometimes people have good intentions and are completely for their marriage, but they express love differently than their partner receives it, and conflict or confusion results.

At the same time, let's say a loving husband brings his wife chocolate. He has a good intention. But the wife has been depressed about her weight. She is cutting candy for her physical and mental wellbeing, and part of this is because she wants to be a happy and attractive spouse. She also is for the marriage, but she doesn't want the chocolate. If the spouses can communicate clearly and recognize their good intentions, the wife will be grateful for the gift instead of feeling like her husband is insensitive. And when she explains why she can't eat it, the husband will be grateful instead of feeling unappreciated. In fact, they'll probably laugh about it.

As a result, healthy intentions result in the building of trust, safety, understanding, and healthy response. Each spouse feels good and confident that whatever situation arises, or whatever problem develops, each spouse is able to trust the other's intentions and seek clear communication. Now who would not want to sign up for that? When both spouses have the intention to understand what or how something is being carried out, this will breed a healthy marriage. As a result, both people are in harmony singing or communicating from the same verse with no doubt that they are into each other and wanting to build intimacy.

For example, let's say you communicate an unhealthy intention of correcting your spouse and this produces fear, avoidance, arguments, demands and hurt. In general, you will start to notice how your spouse will avoid or move away from you. When you correct someone, you seek ways to prove you are right, and your way is correct, and you feel compelled to explain that to the other person. Correcting your spouse is focusing on you. Spouses with unhealthy intentions tend to focus on preserving themselves. In other words, they want to make sure that they are recognized or heard, in order to get some validation or be noticed. They are generally wanting and hoping to get validated to make them feel secure. This will only create a one up/one down relationship similar to an instructor/student relationship.

But the opposite can be said for the people who are seeking healthy intentions. A very important statement that I try to live by and teach others to follow is this: the "we" or "us" is more important than the "me" or "you." Healthy intentions are focused on the relationship and how both people are affected in how they talk and treat one another. People with unhealthy intentions are focused more on "me" or how "I" am individually affected.

When the focus is on the "we" or the two people in the marriage, then the focus is on preserving and valuing the relationship and on loving and respecting one another. When a problem or conflict comes up, the two spouses are focused on how "we" are going to solve it. Unhealthy intentions are focused on how I can make sure I get my point across for the sake of making sure in my arguing, you hear that my way is the right way.

That is why this topic is so important when it comes to how we approach problems and to really understand the intention and goal of where the other person is coming from. Begin to focus on your marriage, take your marriage for a test drive and observe the other person or observe yourself when a conflict comes up, how do both of you attempt to resolve it?

Think "we" and not "me." Focus on not letting any conflict or problem get in the way or allowing hurt and resentment to destroy the "we" relationship. Being in a healthy marriage with two people working side by side and hand in hand on solving relationship problems together is a much healthier approach. You will start to see growth in your own life and in the marriage as two people receive the benefits of love, intimacy, trust, closeness, and confidence so that when a problem arises, you know the two of you can handle it and work together to solve it.

Now that I have talked about the traits of a healthy versus an unhealthy marriage and healthy versus unhealthy intention, please keep on reading and look over these top ten differences between healthy and unhealthy marriages. I hope you are not too discouraged but instead want to know and implement the ten healthy intentions and learn to avoid and get rid of the ten unhealthy intentions. I challenge you to keep on reading so you can make a difference in your marriage and learn how to move from accusing one another to accepting one another.

PART TWO

THE TOP TEN DIFFERENCES

DO YOU WANT THE MARRIAGE TO BE ALL ABOUT YOU OR ALL ABOUT US?

Pre-chapter Quiz: Answer each statement either true or false as it pertains to you.

1. I get angry at my spouse when my ideas are not done my way.

2. I like being independent, and I wish my spouse did not want so much from me.

3. My way of arguing and fighting is to use threatening words.

4. I prefer not to ask for help or be dependent, as I view this as a sign of weakness.

5. My spouse often comments they find me independent and self-reliant.

6. In growing up, no one protected me from harm, so now I act tough to protect myself.

7. I prefer space and feel overwhelmed when my spouse wants something from me.

8. I encourage my spouse for us to be a team and be a "we."

This first difference is a foundation for a healthy marriage. The reality of marriage begins when two people decide to make the relationship about the "we" and not about just the "me." Each person is a "me" before getting married. But the challenge is, now the "me" needs to be put on the back burner for the sake of the "we" or "us" as two married people. In many ways, getting married is the start of focusing less on yourself and now focusing on your spouse and how the two of you are doing as a couple.

UNHEALTHY INTENTION: FOCUS ON YOU

I am not sure exactly why you got married. I am assuming you decided somewhere along the road of life that you wanted a partner or a companion to join you to walk through life. I also am assuming you decided to get married because you did not want to be alone anymore and wanted someone to share life with and be intimate with. At the heart of the matter is a deep human need to love and be loved. In my experience, people do need love and intimacy and do want to connect and be intimate with others for the sake of not feeling alone. Solitude is when you don't mind being focused on yourself, or maybe you are an introvert and are comfortable with yourself and what you

39

Do You Want the Marriage To Be All About You or All About Us?

prefer. Solitude is one thing; loneliness is another thing. Being lonely is painful and may be one of the main reasons you got married in the first place. Choosing to be married is recognizing your need for love and your desire not to be alone anymore.

So now that you are married, it is important to answer and discern this difference: Is the married relationship just about you, or is the marriage about "us." I start with this difference because of the importance and intention of the "we" being and feeling connected and not allowing either part of the "we" to feel alone. When there is a lack of communication and one spouse feels alone in the marriage, due to the other spouse disconnecting (intentionally or not), love and intimacy are hard to maintain. Far too often, marriage today is viewed as, "you be you and I will be me, and if you are asking me to take care of you or be there for you, and this activity interrupts my own personal development, then you are becoming too dependent on me, and that is not what I signed up for."

As a result, more and more marriages are battling this concept of expectations. One spouse has an expectation of taking care of just him or herself, and the other spouse has an expectation of each spouse taking care of the other. For example, let's say Bob feels he wants to focus on taking care of himself while Tracy, his wife, is looking for Bob to take care of her. Bob wishes to be involved with Tracy by being vulnerable and close to her. But if this means he has to give up on his personal desires, feelings and needs, then he will start to pull away from Tracy due to her expectations of him. Tracy went into the marriage focusing on how the "we" are going to meet each other's needs concerning what describes or defines a marriage. Bob went into the marriage somewhat agreeing with Tracy and her ideas, but deep down, he would rather just take care of himself. Love and intimacy becomes confusing and distorted due to the expectations both Bob and Tracy have for the marriage. As a result, they are hurt, disappointed, and frustrated on how to connect.

Bob begins to pull away from Tracy, when she asks him to fulfill her ideas and needs for the "we." Bob is angry, hurt, and resentful towards her due to the pressures of meeting these expectations. As the years go by, Bob decides that the only way to keep going is to focus only on him. He wishes to merge and have a close relationship with Tracy, but given their fighting and disagreements over expectations, Bob is wounded, and the only way he knows to protect and preserve this marriage is to take care of himself. So when the two of them come home from work, dinner is eaten with silence or little conversation, and the rest of the evening is spent with Bob watching ESPN and Tracy on Facebook. Bob tells himself that maybe as the months and years go by, Tracy will start to lower her expectations for the marriage, and the two of them can learn to just accept one another without the expectation to meet each other's needs.

Now the two of them have been married for five years. When Tracy gets together with her girlfriends, they ask how Bob is doing and how she likes

41

Do You Want the Marriage To Be All About You or All About Us?

married life. She shares that she feels Bob is selfish. She begins to describe him as only wanting to focus on himself—he, does not talk or focus on her or the marriage, and she feels alone in this marriage with little connection of love. Tracy does love and pursue Bob, but she feels Bob does not want to be pursued, nor does she experience Bob ever pursuing her. Instead of love and trust, repeated patterns of injuries and intimacy failures have occurred, leaving many scars and hurts. Each spouse now is accusing the other as being selfish and not wanting to be there for the other person. Now Bob and Tracy are viewing each other or the marriage as two people who are more focused on taking care of "me" versus taking care of one another.

Bob reflects on their dating life, their engagement, and their first few years of marriage. He tried to give and help meet Tracy's expectations of being an "us." But the expectations overwhelmed him. He is now empty, frustrated, and exhausted from trying to meet the demands of Tracy's expectations. So his routine of marriage has turned into going away with the guys for a fishing trip, or meeting up with his friends at a sports bar. He now feels taking care of himself is a much better way to function than having to depend or Tracy to meet his needs. His walls are up, as he has concluded that he does not know how to meet her needs, and his initial love for her during the early years has been replaced with only self-preservation. Personal happiness then takes priority over marriage happiness.

As you can see, when this shift happens, of focusing on the "me" instead of the "we," then the marriage will start to break down. Entitlement and selfishness will become more important than meeting the needs of one another. Bob concludes like many people do, that he cannot make her happy, so he is going to focus on making himself happy.

In the above example, I talked about Bob and Tracy, but the roles could have been reversed. I certainly am not out to pick on men or label men as more focused on "me" versus "we." When either the husband or the wife starts to form this conclusion, over time unhealthy patterns will emerge. Each spouse will become unhappy and will look outside of the marriage for their happiness and fulfillment. Temptations may start to emerge, such as flirting with a co-worker, casual cheating, or secretly doing things behind the spouse's back. Far too often, spouses will conclude the grass is greener on the other side of the fence, and they are willing to do what they want for the sake of their entitlement, or because they feel trapped or unable to meet the demands of the "we." Unfortunately, many of today's movies, television shows, and pop culture attitudes tend to affirm this type of thinking.

HEALTHY INTENTION: FOCUS ON US

The shift of focusing on the "we" rather than the "me" starts with assessing trust in the marriage. Focusing on the "we" in the marriage will produce

43

Do You Want the Marriage To Be All About You or All About Us?

high trust. Focusing on "me" in the marriage creates low trust. When trust gets broken as a repeated pattern, selfishness and entitlement will enter the marriage. But when trust is high, there is a better chance for the relationship to focus on the "we." When trust is high, you feel you can begin to talk and share about how you are sensing there is distance in the relationship and you want to find a way to focus on the "we" to preserve the marriage. For a marriage to go the distance, the "we" has to be more important than the "me."

To have the marriage become all about the "we," both spouses need to actively participate in building trust. I often tell couples I counsel that it is just as easy to build a wall of resentment with bricks that have titles on them like hurt, jealousy, anger, bitterness, abandonment, and rejection as it is to build a floor or foundation of trust in which each brick is titled love, empathy, listening, clarifying, honesty, and understanding. "We" spouses focus on each brick, making sure their floor or foundation of trust is firm and strong. "Me" spouses focus on their wall of resentment, justifying their wall and coming up with reasons why they should be or feel resentful. They use this wall of bricks to remain stubborn, distant, hostile, and mean towards their spouse.

Every day, spouses can either build walls of resentment or a foundation of trust in which the marriage becomes stronger with each passing day, week, month and year. Are there going to be holes in the floor of trust? You bet. Occasionally, you are going to need to evaluate the structure and make sure the house is on a cement slab that is strong and hard so it can hold up the house. But "we" spouses don't panic or get bent out of shape when a hole appears. Through the years, they have had enough positive emotional experiences to convince them that trust is high. If you are just starting to build trust, your foundation will be small at first. But if you commit to building the foundation together, you know that you will be there for each other and will help support and build the floor of foundation.

Over time, "we" spouses feel sad and discouraged when a hole appears in their trust floor. A trust brick has been broken and both spouses feel sad this has happened. They quickly look for ways to work together to find another trust brick to fix this hole so their marriage can become strong again.

In "we" marriages, both spouses know they are going to make mistakes. Trusting spouses will be sad and hurt when this happens, but they don't think about building a wall of resentment or look for further evidence why their spouse has let them down, because trust is high. Instead, "we" spouses recognize their spouse has made a mistake, intentionally or not, and trusting spouses will take ownership and responsibility by saying, "my bad, I blew it, I am sorry, I did not mean to hurt you." Trusting spouses will hear this confession, and each will look for ways to build the trust again to repair the brick that has become broken. They are ready to learn from this mistake as a way to build back trust again as they heal the hurt.

45

Do You Want the Marriage To Be All About You or All About Us?

The second area that creates a strong "we" marriage is when both spouses respect one another. To respect one another is to really believe in the other person. When making minor or major decisions, "we" spouses look for ways to hear their spouse's ideas, opinion and feedback. "We" spouses value and like hearing what their spouse has to say and want to hear their ideas or thoughts regarding important decisions that need to be made. When respect is missing, it is difficult to work as a team. If you are feeling indifferent toward your spouse, try to remember what drew you to him or her in the first place. There probably was respect at some point. See if you can make a list of things you respect about your spouse. Tell your spouse what you respect about him or her, and watch for times that character trait comes out. This will help rebuild your respect.

Trust and respect are related. When trust is low, respect is low. When trust is high, there is an active pursuit of wanting to respect each other and their ideas and opinions when it comes to making decisions. You see, respecting one another really comes down to answering this question: "Do you believe in me or us?" When you respect someone, you care about them and believe in them. So, when you are listening to your spouse and sharing your ideas and impressions about a subject, validate what they think and feel. When you believe in someone, what they say counts. Each spouse carefully listens and wants to understand the other person.

As respect grows in the marriage, the "we" becomes stronger, each spouse turns to the other to help make decisions and wants to hear the other's ideas about a project or an investment. So if the family needs a new car, each spouse can do their own research on what they should buy and can sit down at the kitchen table and have a healthy discussion listening and respecting each other's ideas or thoughts on what would be the best car for the family. Each spouse feels included and valued for what they have to say or contribute to make an important decision together!

A final area that I want you to consider when it comes to pursuing a "we" relationship is the important topic of responsiveness. What do I mean when I use this word? Healthy couples who focus on the "we" want to participate as they listen and respond to one another. "We" spouses value learning and growing in the area of how to be sensitive and kind towards one another. When one spouse is speaking, the other spouse is listening with the intention of desiring to respond with kindness, respect, and understanding. How you respond to your spouse when he or she is talking is very important to creating a "we" marriage.

For example, Mario and Amy are having breakfast and reading the newspaper in the morning. Amy is focused on a particular article. She finds having a cup of coffee while reading is the best way to start the day. But then Mario asks her if she has a few minutes as he wants to talk about the day or some event coming up Friday night. A "we"

47

Do You Want the Marriage To Be All About You or All About Us?

response is, "Sure, give me a few minutes while I finish reading this article, and then I can give you my time and attention." With a "we" attitude, Amy will put down the paper, focus, and concentrate on Mario, and will listen and respond to the topic of discussion for the sake of wanting to connect and understand.

The scene changes drastically with a "me" response. Instead of putting down the paper, Amy would say, "Do you have to bring up this topic now? Can't you see I'm reading the newspaper? I do this every morning as this is part of my routine. Why do you have to interrupt my reading in order for me to listen to you? Why does breakfast have to be about talking when all I want to do is read my newspaper in the morning with a cup of coffee! How come you can't join me and also read the paper so there is silence and focus on both of us reading the paper as a way to start our day?"

Mario feels hurt and dismissed. He gets up and walks away in a huff, displaying an angry, cold attitude. Amy says to herself, "Good grief, why does my spouse do this, always wanting to talk to me when I am reading the newspaper? Can't my spouse see I am reading and why does he need to talk to me now?" Amy feels Mario's resentment and then feels hurt by it, causing her to shut down and bury herself further in the paper. Mario is now in the bedroom also reflecting on this encounter and saying, "Here we go again. This is going to be a tough day. She can be so mean in how she responds to me. Why can't she be kind or considerate? Oh well, nothing new, it is all about her all the time. I have to walk on eggshells around her being careful to find the right moment. But boy, if I pick the wrong time, I get this critical response. Why do I feel so often in this marriage that it is all about her?" Mario has now started putting Amy in a box based on her behavior patterns, and he is now less likely to be responsive to her if she does reach out. A lack of responsiveness can create a spiral effect, getting worse and worse.

But healthy or "we" spouses participate together making sure that each spouse feels heard and understood, which can create an upward spiral effect. The more your spouse feels understood, the more he or she will want to confide in you. In the above conversation with Amy and Mario, she could have attempted to negotiate with Mario by asking him to join her in reading the paper in silence with their cups of coffee as a way to start the day. "We" couples look for way to communicate and negotiate so that both spouses feel a win-win proposal and neither one feels like they are being dismissed. "We" spouses do want to work with their spouse and look for ways to compromise so that both spouses feel good about the choices.

The biggest topic in this area of responsiveness is dealing with criticalness. When someone feels criticized, they will usually start to shut down and be quiet. All people and spouses are sensitive to different degrees. It can be helpful to learn when your spouse feels criticized. You may offer a helpful suggestion with an intention of love, but if it hits a

49

Do You Want the Marriage To Be All About You or All About Us?

trigger point for your spouse, he or she could take it as criticism. It happens for both genders, but it may help to be aware that men have strong social pressure to "measure up," and feeling criticized can be devastating for them. To learn about each other, you'll have to tell your spouse (calmly and kindly) when you felt they were critical, and listen to your spouse and be sensitive. "We" spouses make sure when their spouse is speaking, they are attentive, listening, and wanting to respond with warmth and ease without judgment, being critical, or rejecting their spouse.

So the invitation is this: If you really want to make and create a healthy marriage with healthy intentions early on in the dating relationship and in the first few years of marriage, each spouse really does need to clarify and look for evidence that each person in the marriage does want the marriage to be all about the "we" and not just about the "me." Each person is a "me" but for the sake of the other person and for the marriage, each "me" needs to be humble, and suspend their desires for the sake of happiness and emotional and sexual fulfillment that the "we" can create. Marriage is about two spouses becoming a "we." And the most successful couples are able to work together to make a "we" by building trust, respect, and responsiveness.

So look at yourself in the mirror, assess and evaluate how you are doing when it comes to your marriage by asking these questions: "Am I focused on what I want, or am I focused on what we want for our marriage? Am I making all the decisions in the marriage, or are we working as a team to create a strong and healthy marriage by building trust, respect, and healthy responsiveness in our marriage?" When two spouses want and value the "we" versus the "me," the couple is building a foundation of trust for a healthy marriage and future.

Marriage Struggles with a "Me" Focus: What to Do

Now that you have read about this difference, let me share some things you can do to move the marriage from a "me" focus to a "we" focus. The first thing is to write down three to five topics you and your spouse tend to get into arguments over. In this last month, can you recall topics that result in the two of you arguing and fighting? Maybe the topics center on parenting, chores around the house, finances, or arriving late all the time to some event.

Let's use finances as an example. Sit down with your spouse and say, "I notice that we tend to argue about money, and this only leads to the two of us being separate and not working together to manage our money. I want us to do things differently. I don't want us to fight any more about money and the budget. So I am giving you authority to manage our money and to figure out our monthly budget. You seem to think your way is better anyway, so have at it." In general, "me" spouses will want to anyway.

Since your spouse wants their way when it comes to money, allow him or her to be in charge of how the budget and money is spent each month. The

51

Do You Want the Marriage To Be All About You or All About Us?

goal is for you to empower your spouse to manage the money by letting him or her be in charge. Your goal is to allow this to happen for three months and see what happens. Share from your heart that you are tired of all the arguing and you do want to grant him or her permission to oversee the budget.

Spouses who want the focus on them and making the relationship all about "me" deep down are afraid and uncertain of how to do various tasks. You see, all their focus on "me" really is about them not feeling heard or respected. So validate that you do hear and respect them and give the budget to them. My experience is this, after three months, they will find how difficult this is to do, and they will experience frustration and consequences in their life on how to manage the money. Instead of them accusing and complaining about how you manage the money, allow him or her to do it.

Hopefully your "me" spouse will feel the pain and experience the consequences of their strategy for how to do the finances. They are going to make a mistake, and they are going to have troubles. But the goal is not to prove he or she is wrong and you are right, but to allow mistakes and consequences to be the teacher. You may have thought that lecturing, nagging, or yelling would teach your spouse, but that never works. Eventually he or she will need your help managing the finances.

My hope is for you is to use this experience to communicate, in a kind and gentle way, how much you do want "us" working side by side paying the bills together. Emphasize you do not want to fight or argue anymore and your desire is for both of you to participate together, negotiate, and come up with a strategy in which both of you or the "we" are managing the money together.

Marriage Struggles with "We" Focus: What to Do

If you want a healthy relationship focusing on "we," then write out three to five questions you want to ask your spouse. These topics could include love, intimacy, honesty, or trust. Using trust as an example, maybe the first question is this: "What have I done this last week in which I have been earning your trust? Do you experience me as someone who you can trust in my words, behavior, and my response to you? Can you say that I am trustworthy?" Emphasize that your intention and desire is to participate in building a "we" marriage, promising that you will be there for your spouse.

Ask your spouse if there is anything you can do to show him or her you are trustworthy, and ask some ways you can make improvements for the sake of the "we" working as a team. Share your desire to reduce any fears or doubts. You don't want to assume everything is okay in the area of trust. Listen to the feedback, say thanks for the compliments, and ask your spouse to be patient with you if there are some changes he or she would like when it comes to proving you are trustworthy. More than anything, confirm your desire to build trust and intimacy by valuing a focus on the "we." After your spouse gives you feedback, then you also give your spouse appreciation for the ways

53

Do You Want the Marriage To Be All About You or All About Us?

they too participate in trust. To be a strong "we," both spouses need to have regular conversations about trust.

CHAPTER 4
DIFFERENCE #2

DO YOU WANT TO BE RIGHT OR DO YOU WANT TO PURSUE A LOVE RELATIONSHIP?

Pre-chapter Quiz: Answer each statement either true or false as it pertains to you.

1. Today I still live by the standards my parents taught me by trying to do the right thing.

2. Even though I try to please my spouse, I feel it is not good enough.

3. My spouse wants me to do life his or her way, and I feel pressured if I don't.

4. I can share and express areas of disagreement or conflict freely.

5. I don't feel confident that we can resolve conflict without fighting.

6. I tend to argue and have a need to be right when communicating with my spouse.

7. Despite my efforts, I feel I can never do anything right.

8. There are lots of love, affection, and comfort expressed in our marriage.

When you think of your marriage, is it your intention to prove who is right or wrong, and be competitive, or do you want to pursue participating loving one another? You may want both, but feeling the need to be right all the time can get in the way of love. In general, spouses who pursue right and wrong are people who need to be validated for being right.

UNHEALTHY INTENTION: FOCUS ON BEING RIGHT

Let's say Jill is in the kitchen cutting up an onion for a casserole. Her spouse Tom enters the kitchen and observes Jill cutting the onion and says to her, "That is not how you should cut an onion. Here, let me teach you." Now Jill, whose knife has been taken from her, stops and looks over at Tom and says to him, "Why do you always do this? I hate when you come behind me and tell me what I am doing is wrong." Jill becomes defensive due to her feeling that Tom is once again out to remind her, how his way is right and her way is wrong. As you might imagine, Jill and Tom are off, having a heated conversation, and the words are flying. Tom goes into a speech of how Jill's way of cutting the onion is all wrong, and Jill says Tom comes across as Mr. Right, and she feels like Mrs. Wrong in many areas

57

Do You Want To Be Right Or Do You Want To Pursue A Love Relationship?

of their marriage. Tom defends his position and says if that is what Jill feels, maybe it is true. "If the shoe fits, why don't you wear it?"

Jill now storms out of the kitchen. Jill feels that when Tom walks into the house, the whole house braces for him as the children scatter, and she starts to feel the tension of preparing for another point-counterpoint argument regarding something he will point out in order to make it look like he is right and she is wrong.

In fact, Jill intentionally was trying to make Tom's favorite meal for dinner. She was hoping the meal might get the two of them back to being happy. Two days ago they had gotten into another fight over right and wrong, and she was hoping to please him, thinking making his favorite meal might put him in a good mood. She remembers thinking of the fight from a few days ago when he came home and observed the two kids watching television and wanted to know how come they were not doing their homework. Tom insisted they turn off the television as this was wrong and a waste of time. Tom even yelled at Jill when she was in the other room doing some laundry wondering why the kids were watching television when homework needed to be done.

As she was cutting the onion, her mind started to drift back to last Saturday. Her husband Tom was a hard worker and was in sales for a local pharmaceutical company. She thought about how she wanted to surprise him that day by going out to wash his car, and became even more shocked when Tom came out of the house after his Saturday afternoon nap and noticed how Jill was washing the car. Tom again focused on being right, saying Jill was doing it wrong. Tom attempted to say he appreciated her efforts to wash it for him, but he quickly took the sponge out of her hands and told her to go into the house and get dinner ready as he was going to finish washing the car the right way since she was doing it wrong. Jill, once again, felt hurt.

In both examples regarding cutting the onion and washing the car, Tom's intention was to make sure things were done the right way, rather than giving up his way of doing things for the sake of a love relationship. Spouses who push and argue for being right are needing for their spouse to validate their right point of view. When they don't feel validated, they feel hurt given their insecurity of not feeling heard or validated. When spouses like Tom focus on being right, the marriage relationship feels like it is in a court setting. In many ways, the person who is seeking to be right is acting like a judge. Jill feels judged for how she is conducting her life.

Now it might be tempting to minimize right and wrong when it comes to something small like chopping an onion. But what if we apply this right and wrong rule to five important topics in your marriage? Think of the problems of always needing to be right in these areas: 1) intimacy, 2) parenting, 3) managing money, 4) house chores, and 5) your choice of friends. It saddens me as a therapist when I view the battles two spouses are having

59

Do You Want To Be Right Or Do You Want To Pursue A Love Relationship?

in their fight for who is right. When one spouse is out to prove they are right, and the other spouse is defensive and also trying to prove they are right, it is like a tug of war. The battle is like a tennis match where both people are smashing the ball, or topic, back and forth right in front of me, thinking that I will judge or find favor in one person's logical points.

When spouses view the marriage arena like a competition, a power struggle ensues, and love and trust gets traded for proving a point. Now I am all for competition and for doing your best, and for excellence in all that we do. People often attempt to reach and attain high goals in their careers or hobbies, and this is fine. But marriage was never designed to be the place for competition. Love says, "I want to be with you." Competition and power says, "I want to win and beat you in this game."

So answer these questions: Have you noticed that you or your spouse are trying to prove who is right and who is wrong, and how is that going for you? Is it working? Would you be willing to be wrong sometimes in order to have a better relationship with your spouse? Is proving you are right and your spouse wrong bringing closeness and harmony between the two of you? Can you see how proving you are right is leading to accusations in which in your accusing, you are pointing out how your spouse is wrong and you are right?

If you are in a marriage with someone whose intention is to be right, let me go deeper in attempting to explain where this spouse may be coming from. In general, someone who is out to prove she or he is right is deeply afraid of being perceived as being a failure. Avoiding failure and seeking perfection is the drive behind the need to be right. Not only do they want to be right and affirmed for being right, but they also want you to follow their ideas about how to do something right. Maybe they grew up with a parent who was tough on them, or maybe they grew up with siblings where there was competition and criticism. At the core is this belief: If I am not validated for being right, then I feel dismissed or may feel like a failure. In other words, they have never felt validated or given permission that it is okay to not be right or that life has to go their way all the time.

For example, I heard the story of a couple who went out to dinner to a nice restaurant. The husband had been away on a business trip and had not seen his wife for a few days. His wife was excited to also see him and she scheduled reservations at a new restaurant they had wanted to try out. Half way into their meal their conversation led to what spice was being used for a particular dish. The husband argued it was one spice while the wife proposed it was another spice.

To settle this debate, the husband asked their waitress to ask the cook what is the particular spice that was being used in this one dish. The waitress asked the cook and the husband's point or spice, proved to be right, and he did a little dance in his chair celebrating his victory that he was right or he had won.

61

Do You Want To Be Right Or Do You Want To Pursue A Love Relationship?

Needless to say, the wife was hurt. She shut down, said very little the rest of the night, and the evening was filled with more silence than words. She ended up going to bed early with little time spent in any romance or intimacy. Arguing the point of what spice was used in a particular dish certainly led to the husband being right. But in the end, the wife was hurt and annoyed over how much the husband was so proud of being right and how little love and intimacy they had given each other due to his need to be right. Trying to win so your spouse loses by proving you are right is a recipe for hurt and defeat.

Healthy Intention: Focus on Being Loved

When you play tennis with your spouse, both of you are hitting the ball back and forth. If you are focused on being right, you will stay on opposite sides of the net. But those spouses who are pursuing a love relationship will want to come over to the side of the net where there spouse is and say, "Hey, can we be a team? Can't we both be on this side of the net and work together for the sake of the relationship? Let's try to find another couple we can play with and enjoy some good exercise!"

Seeking a love relationship is about giving up your need to be right and just wanting to be close and be with the other person. The goal is teamwork, not competition. No one wants someone to come behind them and observe their choices and judge how they do things. What Jill really wanted was for Tom to grab a utensil and work alongside her in the kitchen or grab a rag and join her in washing the car.

Healthy marriages are built on the intention that when they are together, talking or working on a project, they feel like the other person is on their side. The "we" again becomes more important than the "me." Healthy spouses act as a team parenting their children, discussing their budget, doing chores around the house, and relating in the bedroom.

Let's face it: both spouses need love. Both spouses need their spouse to love them just as they are with their strengths and weakness, for better or worse. Spouses are tired of being judged and tired of having to prove their point all the time. All this activity is exhausting. In other words, spouses who want to pursue a love relationship recognize their need for love and make it a higher priority than being right. When you give love and when you receive love, you form a close and intimate relationship. Healthy people pursue love because they want lots of trust, lots of empathy, and lots of intimacy.

Maybe you want both. Maybe you are thinking that you would like love and intimacy, but you also want to be right all the time. If you are afraid of feeling like a failure, consider this: biting your tongue when you want to correct your spouse may actually be a way to succeed. Holding back criticism and admitting you're wrong can help you win. You may not win the argument, but you're much more

63

Do You Want To Be Right Or Do You Want To Pursue A Love Relationship?

likely to win your spouse's affection. If you want to be right, you may not be aware how much this can affect your spouse. You were likely criticized a lot at some point in your life. Do you remember how it felt? You probably don't want to make your spouse feel that way. If you've gotten used to criticizing, it will take time to break the pattern.

Spouses who want love also want safety. They want to feel free, not to walk on eggshells, and feel accepted for who they are. They feel safe and secure with someone who loves them and who wants to pursue being loved. So try being honest with your spouse about your vulnerable feelings and fears, and try to catch yourself when you feel the need to be right. It is a difficult change to make, but it is possible. Remember, proving you are right breeds fear and insecurity. Pursuing love breeds trust and safety. Love conquers being right, and love wins. To be right hurts your marriage. But to pursue love heals your marriage. Find a way to stop the accusing and learn to find a way to work with your spouse on building a love relationship.

Marriage Struggles with Being Right: What to Do

The invitation for a spouse who is married to someone who insists on being right is to invite them out for breakfast or for a cup of coffee. For the discussion, begin with affirming him or her for being your spouse and list all the things your spouse does that are right. Compliment them for all the ways they do things right and how you respect their desire to do the right thing.

In addition, become vulnerable, expressing kindness and gratitude for how your spouse has to put up with you. Say how you feel lucky to have him or her, given all the mistakes you tend to make. Share with your spouse how much you want to learn how to do things right, and you want to respect their need to be heard by considering their ideas and suggestions.

Then ask your spouse to affirm you, describing how your spouse respects and appreciates you. Ask in what areas you do things right, and how that makes them feel. Remind your spouse you are not perfect and how they must be patient for putting up with you, given you do make mistakes.

Then ask this question: "Is there room in our marriage for each of us daily to admit one mistake each person made that day? Can we confess what we did wrong today?" Share an example of how you felt when you made a certain mistake and how this affected your stress and frustration level. Remind your spouse how you tend to have a harsh conscience and sometimes beat yourself up for making a mistake.

After sharing about yourself, ask your spouse what one mistake they made and how they responded and felt about making this mistake. Were they also harsh on themselves, and how did it affect their stress and frustration level? Could they notice they felt stressed, angry, and frustrated when they made the mistake?

The goal is this: invite your spouse to normalize mistakes. It is normal for us to make mistakes.

65

Do You Want To Be Right Or Do You Want To Pursue A Love Relationship?

State you would like each day to spend ten minutes to share and confess, with honesty and vulnerability, areas in which both of you make mistakes and how it affects not only each other but the marriage. Can you both value and desire confessing your mistakes as a way to recognize how both of you are imperfect? Does it feel okay to admit this? Remind your spouse that you do want to self-correct, but more than anything, you want to feel loved and accepted when either of you makes a mistake. Invite your spouse to participate in this activity and over time, see what happens.

Marriage Struggles with Love: What to Do

The goal for this section is to focus on reducing the stress and anxiety in your marriage. Trying to be right, in control, and managing life to go the right way can be stressful for your spouse. Moving from being right to partnering in a love relationship means finding ways to help your spouse not feel so stressed and anxious all the time.

So, have this conversation with your spouse: "Tell me honey, how are you reducing stress in your life? What are some things you do that help you become relaxed, have fun, and be silly? I know you are highly responsible, and you try to help us do the right thing. So I would love to support you in areas in which you can feel relaxed, have fun, be silly, and laugh. What can I do to help you relax and reduce the stress in your life? Tell me some ways in which I can help you find laughter and have fun again." Hopefully, you both will participate in doing things that are fun and silly.

In other words, get into your spouse's world and share how you want to help balance out the stress and tension with some suggestions for fun, laughter, and relaxation. For example, maybe the two of you love music and dancing. Can you both find the time to do this twice a month so you both are laughing, relaxing, engaging in activities of fun and laughter?

Cultivate and think of ways to engage in fun and relaxation, as this will greatly increase the love between the two of you. I promise you this: reduced stress will increase the possibilities for a deeper love relationship. Remind your spouse there is a time to be right and there is a time to relax, have fun, make mistakes, and be silly. Marriages that thrive focus on a love relationship involve two people reducing stress and having more fun.

DO YOU WANT TO CORRECT
OR DO YOU WANT TO ACCEPT?

Pre-chapter Quiz: Answer each statement either true or false as it pertains to you.

1. When my spouse fails or makes a mistake, I react with anger and frustration.

2. It does not bother me that my spouse has to walk on eggshells around me.

3. I feel if I don't do something correctly according to my spouse, I will be threatened.

4. When my spouse asks me how I feel, I do get uncomfortable and just say "fine."

5. In our marriage, communicating and saying kind words to each other is infrequent.

6. I try to do things right in order to keep the peace in this marriage.

7. I often feel accused or ignored when I make a mistake.

8. My spouse knows my strengths and weaknesses and still accepts me.

How would you define correction? As a society, we view this as attempting to fix something or someone who has done something wrong or who has made a mistake. To correct is to remove an error or fault to become true or accurate. To correct an action is to do something to reverse or fix a mistake or inaccuracy.

UNHEALTHY INTENTION: FOCUS ON CORRECTING

We all use a device called a pencil. A pencil has on one end the lead to write and on the opposite end an eraser to correct. The pencil has built into its system both the ability to write and to correct. To write is to use the lead, to correct is to use the eraser. I don't know who invented this instrument, but they assumed accurately that one was going to make a mistake and built in to the device an eraser to correct the mistake. Now isn't that interesting? There are things in life that have built into them a system to give you a second chance. As I am typing this, I have the tool to delete or backspace or correct something I typed.

But when we think of marriage, we cannot apply this same principle. Each spouse can and should self-correct, but far too often spouses take on the role of correcting their husband or wife. Let me ask you this: When you got married, were you signing up for your spouse to correct you? Do you feel marriage is the place where it is okay for the role of a spouse to correct one another? When speaking your vows, did you promise to correct one another?

Think back to the last week. Did you make a mistake in your marriage last week? When you made this mistake, how did your spouse react? Can you make a mistake without the fear that your spouse is out to correct you? Are you living in fear that you will make a mistake and your spouse will use this opportunity to rush in and try to correct you? Do you feel the need to correct your spouse?

Let's say you drop the glass vase in the living room or you get distracted and overcook the meatloaf in the oven. Does your spouse make correcting comments of how in the future you should not break things or burn things? Does your spouse feel the right to correct you? To correct a meatloaf from getting burnt in the future is to correct how you do something, but if your spouse also feels your character needs to be corrected, now your spouse has crossed the line if they call you stupid or dumb for burning the meatloaf. The meatloaf not getting burnt is one thing, fixing and correct you the person is another thing.

To correct one another will lead to an unhealthy pattern in a marriage. On your wedding day, you vowed to love each other for better or for worse. To love is to accept. But in a correcting marriage, each spouse does not accept the other's "worse." When spouses conclude it is their responsibility to fix or correct you, you then run into the trouble of feeling you are not loved or accepted for better or worse.

For example, let's say one spouse backs out the car from the garage and accidently hits something that results in the car getting scratched or bruised. This spouse feels guilty and remorseful for damaging the car. They feel sad, and later in the day they explain to their spouse what happened. How will the spouse respond? Will he or she say, "That's okay honey, you have not been injured, the car has been injured, and it is not a big deal. I forgive you, and I know it was an accident." That would be a healthy, intentional, and accepting response. But let's look at another response: "What? How could you do this? I have told you to be careful when backing up this car. I even gave you instructions to show you how to back out the car from the garage so you don't scratch it. What was your thinking? How could this happen?"

Now the driver of the car is not only feeling guilty, he or she is feeling embarrassed or maybe even shameful and bad. The result of the correction is to make the spouse feel shame. Guilt says you accidently made a mistake. Shame says you made a mistake, and you are a mistake. Shame says you need to be fixed and corrected. This then leads to hurt feelings or verbal abuse and the sting of your spouse's words. Verbal abuse is common, and when the correcting spouse uses his or her words to shame you, put you down, and make you feel bad and shameful for making a mistake, the long-term verbal and emotional abuse will affect the hurting spouse for months or even years.

Sometimes people correct because they think that is the only way their spouse will learn a lesson in life. Sometimes it is the result of a bad day or a problem not related to the spouse. If you realize you've slipped up and corrected your spouse recently, you can own your mistake and apologize. We may mean well when we correct our spouses, but this is the message we send: "I will love you and accept you if you are good; but I will be out to correct and shame you if you are bad." Spouses will start to make this conclusion: If I am good, I will not get corrected and can earn my spouses favor by not making a mistake. When conditions enter a marriage, spouses play games with each other.

That is why this topic is so important for marriage. If one spouse frequently corrects the other, affection becomes conditional based on behavior. The receiving spouse will come to know this unspoken rule and will become cautious and perhaps withdrawn and anxious. This unspoken rule of conditional love and acceptance happens a lot in marriages, and people hope to please their spouse by trying not to make any mistakes. If love and acceptance is not free, then love and acceptance must be earned. To earn means you have to perform for my love and acceptance. Be good and minimize your mistakes and I will love you more. If you are not good, and make mistakes, I will love you less and also take on the role of correcting you.

Imagine how it feels to always be looking over

your shoulder, fearing your spouse will pounce on you to point out you made a mistake. If you are in the habit of correcting, you may not even realize how difficult it is for your spouse. If you feel like you are holding your breath all the time waiting for the next blow, you may, have a spouse who is in the mode of correcting. Can you see if this happens over and over how much this can hurt a person and hurt the marriage?

We live in a society that is constantly looking for fault, wanting answers when people make a mistake, and attempting to connect the dots to come up with an explanation for how or why everything happens. To relate to people means you are relating to mistakes. Correcting spouses are impatient and point out mistakes that leaves the other spouse feeling they have to justify themselves. They are like detectives looking for evidence not only to correct the problem but also you.

If your intention and goal is to look for problems or mistakes and try to correct them, you will never be satisfied or happy. I often tell correcting spouses they should get a fish tank with a goldfish as this may satisfy them. Fishes do not make mistakes and all they need is some basic food. In general, goldfish do not need correction because all they is a little food. But cars, machines, dogs, cats and humans will let you down and may never satisfy you as they make mistakes.

Healthy Intention: Focus on Accepting

Do you remember the words from Billy Joel's famous song: "I Love You Just the Way You Are?[1]" He wrote and sang: "Don't go changing to try and please me, you never let me down before; I'll take the good times; I'll take the bad times, I'll take you just the way you are." The singer is pleading his lover not to change; he wants her exactly as she is. Can you relate to this song? If you've fallen into a habit of correcting, can you remember a time when you just wanted to pursue your spouse and adore everything about them? Accepting one another means you want to love and support someone for better or worse, for richer or poor, in sickness and in health. These vows made on your wedding day are statements that you do want love and you do want acceptance, and you want to give them to your spouse.

Being accepting does not mean you are closed to hearing a correction. It just depends who is the one correcting, and the intention. We all need to self-correct and learn from our mistakes. It is healthy to say to our spouse, "My bad, I blew it, and I apologize for this. I am sorry." Hopefully in healthy marriages, the intention is to accept one another and receive this apology.

For example, let's say Julie decides to take tennis lessons. She hires a tennis coach to teach her how to swing the backhand correctly to hit the ball consistently over the net. The coach's intention is to teach and train Julie to correct her swing by making sure her arms or legs are in the right position. Julie accepts this correction because she has hired this coach to correct her swing. But what would happen if this coach started to not only correct her backswing but starts to correct her. For example, if this coach starts to attack her character, starts to accuse her of being lazy or stupid, then the tennis coach is moving past his role as a tennis coach and is now trying to correct Julie, which is not what she hired him to do.

So Julie feels hurt and angry because this coach is now mean attacking her character. She comes home and tells her husband what this coach said and how she feels about this. An accepting spouse would provide some empathy and understanding for Julie. A correcting spouse would agree with the coach and affirm that Julie is lazy and not too smart, and she should by now know how to execute a backhand. The correcting spouse goes on to say that he feels she is wasting money and time and even questions why she even signed up for a coach in the first place. Now how does Julie feel? Does she feel supported and loved, or does she feel she now has two men in her life who are out to correct her. Does her character really need to be corrected?

When you decide to marry someone, you are not choosing your spouse to be your coach, to be your mentor, to ask of them to fix or correct you regarding a mistake or problem in your life. You married for love and acceptance, not for being fixed and corrected. What would it look like in the marriage ceremony if the spouses said to one another that they know they are broken, they will make mistakes, and they are vowing to accept one another and not correct one another? All you want is to be loved and to be accepted. Acceptance is so important to relationship, allowing you to walk in confidence that your spouse will not rush in to punish, correct, or go into a rage every time you make a mistake.

This reminds me of insurance companies which offer accident forgiveness. The companies advertise that they will be there when you make a mistake or accident, and thus, are accepting and providing forgiveness. In a healthy marriage, a mistake is not the end of the world but an opportunity for forgiveness and learning.

Pointing Out Unhealthy Behavior with Loving Intention

You may be asking then this question: Am I to accept my spouse who chooses habits or activities that hurt me? How do I deal with this? Am I to sit back and be passive and just accept my spouse who consistently hurts me and the marriage and doesn't want to correct the way they hurt me?

When Tina and Bill dated, she worried about Bill and his drinking habits. She liked him and found him to be funny. They would go out to a bar, drink, and laugh together. They decided to get married, and their first year was filled with lots of love, laughter, and fun. Both had stressful jobs but were committed to their work, and both felt good about the companies they worked for. In their first few years, Tina started to notice a pattern that was becoming problematic. Bill needed his beer every day. Tina liked to drink, and it helped her calm down, but she also noticed that she could go without some wine or mixed drink for a few days. But not Bill. He seemed to need and want to drink beer every day.

As time went by, Tina started to pay more attention to how much money was being spent on both of their drinking. She started to wonder, what if they were to limit their budget for drinks. She proposed this one day to Bill, and he replied that she worried too much and needed to relax. Besides, he said, he had already begun taking lunch to work and making his own coffee in the morning rather than going out to his favorite coffee place. Bill figured he could spend money on beer since he had made sacrifices in other areas. He told Tina he would start buying beer in the 12 pack or 24 pack at Costco to save money. Tina reluctantly went along with this idea.

Tina also rationalized that at least Bill was just drinking at home. But then he went to the sports bar one night with some of his buddies and got drunk. Bill could not control his drinking, did not have a designated driver, and got a DUI on the way home from the restaurant. When Bill got home, Tina was furious. How could he be so irresponsible and put his life in danger?

Tina feared that her husband was turning into an alcoholic. Sure, he could work, and he was functional, but his mood, feelings, and attitude would change when he drank, and Tina not only worried about his drinking but was beginning to worry about their marriage. Tina continued to try to correct him with her nagging and criticism of his drinking, but her words only led to Bill pulling away from her, and she now felt even more alone in the marriage concluding Bill was more interested in drinking his beer and watching sports than spending time with her. She sought out a therapist so she could share her personal pain and conflict over what to do.

The therapist suggested Tina have a conversation with Bill regarding alcohol in the marriage, saying something like this: "Honey, I love you and I accept you. I accept your choice to drink, and I accept you as a person who drinks. But, what I cannot accept is the money you spend on drinking because now we don't have enough money to pay the electric bill, and the electric company is going to turn off our electricity this Friday. I also know that I accept and love you for better or for worse, but when you drink, you change, and you become mean and hurtful to me. Is there any way that you could see how beer and you drinking beer affects me and how much it hurts us? Can we both find ways to understand, accept, and decide together if beer is something that we both want in this marriage?"

The goal and intention for Tina is to share her experience of how Bill's drinking is affecting her and their marriage without trying to correct and change Bill. We can never ever, change or correct someone else. We can only change ourselves by asking this question: When I have a problem, not only how does this problem affect me, but how does this problem affect my spouse? Tina wants to know how Bill feels that his drinking not only affects her and the marriage but is also asking Bill does it bother him that his wife is hurt, sad, scared, and anxious. These feelings affect Tina but do these feelings affect Bill and does he feel anything or does he feel sad that his wife has these feelings? It is not the job of spouses to change each other, but they can act as mirrors, helping each other see areas of needed change. It is important that the intention is loving, not correcting, and there is still acceptance of the spouse as a person.

In other words, accept the person but not the problem, and learn ways to have good boundaries to help protect yourself. You cannot set a boundary on someone else by trying to control them and tell them what to do. If you think you can correct, change, fix or solve your spouse's problems, you are setting yourself up for a life of unhealthy patterns and misery. All you can do is set limits to how much exposure you want to have when he or she does these things. If someone in your life is acting out and hurting you, try to work with them on solving this problem, i.e., alcohol in the marriage, but move away from the person and inform them you are moving away not because you hate them or don't accept them. But you are moving away from them because trying to fix, correct, or change them is not working and will never work. Tina needs to explain to Bill how his drinking affects her and invite him to work together on the problem. She is on his team, but it's up to him to swing the bat. Be a team member, not an angry, correcting, fixing or changing spouse.

Think of it this way. What if Tina gets diagnosed with Stage III ovarian cancer? Both alcoholism and cancer are diseases that you cannot just flip the switch and fix overnight. Being diagnosed with cancer is very frightening and very challenging. Tina is going to have to participate in many forms of cancer treatment to remove this cancer from her body. Hopefully, Bill will be loving and supportive and will want to work with Tina on this problem. Tina has cancer, not Bill, but cancer now has entered the marriage, and they both need to be a team and a "we" to fight this deadly disease. Bill cannot sit back and say, "This is your problem, you have cancer, I don't, so you need to fix it alone, be responsible, and take care of it yourself."

In the same way, alcohol, drugs, pornography, financial irresponsibility, anger, abuse and other acting out behaviors are like cancer. Cancer is not good for a marriage, and alcoholism is also not good for a marriage. The bottom line is this, all marriages need to be a "we" or a team. If your spouse gets cancer, both of you need to work together to conquer cancer together. If there is a water leak at your house and the kitchen gets flooded, both spouses need to work together to solve this problem. If your spouse has a drinking problem, both of you have a problem, and both of you need to work together to solve it together. That is healthy.

Loving and accepting one another means you will talk and work together without the need to nag, yell, blame, or correct. Those strategies will not work. Instead invite your spouse to work with you so that the two of you are solving life's problems together out of acceptance and not out of correction.

Marriage Struggles with Correcting: What to Do

If you find you are in a marriage with a spouse who wants to correct, my heart goes out to you. Being married to someone with the intention of wanting to correct can lead to you feeling like you have to walk on eggshells. The challenge for you is to find a way not to walk in fear anymore.

How do you do this? You will need to value honest confrontation. This means you do not focus on the topic your spouse wants corrected, but instead focus the conversation on how you are feeling and are affected by being corrected. Find the courage to express your voice and not be afraid to share your feelings. And the most important feeling I want you to share is hurt. Not anger, not fear, but hurt. When you feel hurt, express these words: "Ouch that hurts."

As a child, you probably used these words when you felt hurt. But now as an adult, you also get hurt. And this hurt is from the person you love and married. And now you need to say to the one you love, "You hurt me." When you can say this on a regular basis and be honest about the hurt and sad feelings you are experiencing, then you are ready to help your spouse understand how his or her correcting words hurt you. When you are able to say how sad you feel and how you want to pull away and not talk to him or her, maybe your spouse will not like you feeling sad and pulling away. This is the first step toward change.

As you know, a happy spouse means a happy married life. But a sad spouse can mean an unhappy married life. As a result, you will need to share and say, "Ouch that hurts! When you are focused on correcting me in your words and tone of voice, this hurts and makes me feel sad. And being sad means I don't want to be close to you, and I want to be quiet around you. So this weekend, I think it would be a good idea for us to be separate and say little. You go and do what you want to do, and I will do what I want to do."

Say these words and be honest with your spouse about how hurt and sad you are feeling. Hopefully your correcting spouse will be sad that you're hurt and will want to change. Help your spouse understand that you will not tolerate being corrected, as his or her words hurt you, resulting in you shutting down and wanting to be left alone. Hopefully, your spouse does not want this and will want to work with you on reducing correction in your marriage.

Marriage Struggles with Accepting: What to Do
To work towards a healthy marriage wanting acceptance means for each spouse to decide to

accept one another for better or for worse. So make a list of the top five worst character flaws and habits your spouse engages in and ask yourself this question: Can I really find a way to accept these irritating habits? Can I find a way to not react and not make a correcting comment about my spouse?

To accept means you are not out to fix or change your spouse. So sit down with your spouse and communicate how much you do want acceptance in this marriage. Ask your spouse if they feel accepted in this marriage. Ask if you have done anything this last week in which your spouse has not felt accepted. If so, ask, "How did this affect you, and how do you feel about me and our marriage?"

Say to your spouse: "I really want us to value learning how to accept one another instead of us trying to fix or correct one another! My goal is for us to find a way to accept one another despite the fact that I am sure there are traits about me that you find difficult. So why don't we do this? Why don't you tell me your top five preferences, and I will tell you my top five preferences. I know that you prefer milk and sugar in your coffee, and I like flavored creamer and sweetener in my coffee. Because we love one another, can we find a way to meet each other's preferences? Can we find a way to accept one another's preferences so we can learn to accept each other?"

By having this conversation with your spouse, you are inviting your spouse to participate in building a healthy relationship for the sake of valuing acceptance. Have this conversation and look for ways to move from correcting one another to accepting one another.

DO YOU WANT TO CRITICIZE
OR DO YOU WANT TO ENCOURAGE?

Pre-chapter Quiz: Answer each statement either true or false as it pertains to you.

1. I try to keep my spouse happy so he or she will not criticize me.

2. I long for connection and attention from my spouse but end up feeling empty.

3. I am not a moody person, and I get irritated when my spouse is emotional.

4. I prefer life to be predictable and avoid taking risks so I will not be criticized.

5. Despite my efforts to please, I often feel alone, unloved, and neglected by my spouse.

6. I feel my spouse seeks out my opinion and cares about my feelings.

7. I am able to show affection and words of encouragement to my spouse.

8. My spouse knows my gifts and talents and encourages me to use them.

How would you define criticism? How does it feel to experience someone criticizing you? Do you like it, or does it hurt you? When you were a child, can you remember a time when a parent criticized you, and how that made you feel? As a spouse in your marriage, how does it feel when your spouse is critical of you? How do you feel when your spouse encourages you? Do you like and value being encouraged or being an encourager in your marriage?

UNHEALTHY INTENTION: FOCUS ON BEING CRITICAL

The world is full of opinions and criticism. If you watch television, there are many different shows in which people participate in a competition and someone judge's contestants based upon some certain criteria. When you watch the Olympics, the athletes are competing against one another, and there is a judge who is observing their participation and judging them on their skills. In addition to sports, there are competitions for cooking, singing, dancing, training animals, and more.

To be a critic, usually someone has achieved some level of expertise, and they are quali-fied to judge. When you are watching a music competition, such as 'American Idol' or 'The Voice,' you will notice the judges are musicians qualified to be a critic of the contestants who are attempting to win this competition. The critic usually is qualified when it comes to music given they have attained some level of fame as a musician.

For years, one of the early pop culture television shows was "Siskel and Ebert" who weekly gave their critical views of new movies opening in local theaters. They would give either a thumbs up or down regarding whether the viewing audience should go and spend their money on a particular movie. What qualified them to be movie critics was each of them attained this title given they worked at a newspaper as a film critic. Each week millions would watch this show to catch a view or rating on an upcoming movie. The show became very famous.

In general, critics are professionals with some level of talent, expertise, or knowledge which qualifies them to sit in the judge's seat. If you were a contestant in a singing contest, you would want Jenifer Lopez to be judging the talent of the singers and not me. I certainly am not qualified as an expert when it comes to judging singing.

But when we apply this description of being a critic to a marriage, unhealthy patterns can start to hurt the marriage if one spouse concludes they are qualified to judge you as a spouse. For example, consider the weekly television show "All in the Family" that ran successfully for many years on television. Viewers laughed at the critic, Archie

Bunker. He criticized his wife, daughter, son-in-law, and others. People laughed at how he would make fun of people, yell and scream at his family, or judge others behind their back and make derogatory comments about them, attempting to put them down and make him look good. Archie used criticism to be mean and hurtful, engaging in arguments and fights with his family, especially his son-in-law Mike (who he called "Meathead") and his wife Edith (who he called a "Dingbat").

On television, this may be funny. But in your marriage, this is not funny, as being critical of your spouse does hurt. To be a critic in a dog show is one thing; to be a critic of your spouse's cooking, that is another thing. In marriage, no one wants to be criticized or verbally abused with mean, hurtful words coming from the person you thought loved you and cared about you. Critical people hurt people.

If your intention is to be critical, you will cause lots of hurts and distrust in your marriage. You see, all people are sensitive. We are all sensitive to someone judging or criticizing us. This sensitivity probably stems from childhood when someone was a bully to us, made fun of us, or was mean to us, and all these hurts never got healed. Marriage is supposed to be a place in which you ask your spouse to love you, accept and encourage you, and find ways to be patient and kind to you. Certainly one does not say yes to marriage, asking for their spouse to spend the rest of their married life criticizing them. We are all sensitive people, and we need our spouse to encourage us and be our biggest fan, and not our biggest critic.

So when you are critical, you are adding hurts to hurting people who are sensitive to words of criticism. Our mouth and our tongue can get us into trouble if we feel free to just say what we want and we have no filter over our mouth in what or how we say some words. Consider the worlds of Facebook, Twitter and Instagram in which one feels free to type or text what they think or feel. Unfortunately, these modern technical devices can be used to hurt others. I am all for freedom of speech, but I am not for freedom of speech in a marriage when spouses misuse this freedom to hurt people with their words. Oftentimes, hurt happens when one spouse will say they are just being honest, and they justify their position of being free to give their opinions and criticism.

We all need to be careful putting ourselves in a position of authority when we really are not in a position to judge or criticize. If we go around each day and look for ways to give our opinion, observe what someone is doing, and decide to criticize, it is almost like we are watching our spouse and looking for ways to fix them. Sometimes if criticism is confronted, the one who criticized will say, "That is your problem and not mine." In other words, if someone reacts or does not like how they get criticized, the critical spouse often feels it is the other person's issue. They think their spouse is too sensitive, that they need to grow a tougher skin and deal with it, and for the most part they justify their critical comments as only giving their opinion, "If you can't handle the truth, well, that's your problem."

When someone sign's up for the army, they know they will get criticized by a sergeant or person in authority who is out to shape and criticize them, molding the person to be a good soldier. If someone takes lessons from Tiger Woods teaching this person how to hit a 5 iron, they would expect him to be critical. But when you are married, you did not sign up for your spouse to be your sergeant.

So all of us need to be careful in how we talk and treat one another. We all need to answer this question: Am I really an expert and an authority in this area to place myself in a position to be a critic? If you want to be a film critic, go to film school and learn all about the world of filming. But in your marriage, take off that critic hat and figure out a way to encourage your spouse. Because as you do this, the one being criticized will become less defensive, and the two of you will create a safe relationship and not a place where hurt and battle happens due to one spouse feeling as if they are a failure.

HEALTHY INTENTION: FOCUS ON ENCOURAGING

How would you define encouragement? How does it feel to be an encourager? Have you ever known someone who encouraged you? How did it feel to hear words of encouragement? When you hear words of encouragement, does it cause you to draw closer to the encourager?

If there is one thing that is true it is this: If you hear words of criticism from your spouse, you will move away or not want to be close to them. But if you hear words of encouragement, you will move towards them and want to be close to them. Critical words and statements sabotage intimacy and closeness, but encouraging words build intimacy. Critical people demand something from you, while encouraging people cheer you on to do your best. When you struggle, encouraging people feel you can do better and work alongside you to help you make some improvements. Encouraging people don't stand on the sidelines but jump right in with sensitive, kind, and cheerful words, thinking of ways to work with you so you can do your best.

Critical people are like cactus plants. If you go to the dessert and walk around a cactus plant, you more than likely are not going to go up and give it a hug. The thorns on these plants really do hurt, and hugging a cactus plant hurts. Sure, the cactus flower can be pretty to look at from a distance, but to get close, you may get hurt by the thorns.

Encouraging people are like a rose bush. Encouraging people do have thorns—we all have thorns—but, the flower, leaves, and plant are so beautiful that you do want to get close, and the thorns don't cause you to pull away. The beauty and smell of the rose draws you in to be close and smell the flower, and you are careful not to allow the thorns to hurt you. You see, the healthy intention of wanting to be an encourager really does build healthy marriages. We all know that we can be our own worst enemies, and we can all be critical of ourselves. So we really don't need someone else to come along and add more words of criticism to our sensitive self-worth. What we all need is someone to encourage us, as this really does say this person believes in me.

Think about a tough day you had recently. Maybe you had a tough day at work, or had car problems, or got into a fight with your child or a friend. At the end of the day, what did you need from your spouse? Do you need to hear someone be critical of you for your thinking, decision making, or actions that day? Are you really needing critical comments pointing out where you went wrong and what you should have done differently? Is that really what you are needing to hear? Hopefully after you have had a bad day, your spouse will listen, care, and give you words of encouragement. To encourage someone is to inspire them with courage, confidence, and words of care. People who encourage are positive; they say words to foster an environment for a safe and trusting relationship. All people need encouragement and encouraging words.

Do you remember the words of Kenny Rodgers song "She Believes in Me?[2]" I have to admit, when I heard that song years ago, it really rang true for me, as I could relate to those words of how this man felt regarding a woman who believed in him. The main words to the song are the following: "And she believes in me, I'll never know just what she sees in me, I told her someday if she was my girl, I could change the world with my little song, but I was wrong. But she has faith in me, and so I go on trying faithfully. And who knows maybe on some special night, if my song is right, I can find a way, while she waits for me."

When you are an encourager, you are saying to your spouse that you believe in them, desire to care for them, and show words of care and kindness to them. When you are critical, you view life as a 100-yard dash, and you feel the need to quickly rush in and try to fix or inform someone where they went wrong. But an encourager sees life as a long marathon journey in which we all need someone on the sidelines of life cheering us on, believing in us, and telling us we can make it.

To be an encourager is similar to being a cheerleader. If you watch a college football game and you observe the cheerleaders on the side, they are encouragers. Whether the team is winning or losing, cheerleaders are out to cheer them on and believe in them, whether they are winning or losing. Even if the team is losing and the score in the 4th quarter is 42-7, the cheerleaders still boost the team and the fans in the stands to keep on supporting their team. To be encouragers is to be one another's biggest cheerleaders. We all are going to have good days and bad days, and we need someone, in life to be our encourager.

In marriage, we want someone who we can come home to who will be an encourager, who will cheer us on, and will want to walk and stand by us as we find ways to do life. As a spouse, after you have worked all day or gone to school all day, you need to take off your work or student hat and come home and be with someone who wants to be your friend, your cheerleader, someone who believes in you and wants to give you words of encouragement. Choose to believe in your spouse and cheer them on. Shake off the critics and find people who desire to believe in you and encourage you. Because when they do this, and as you give it back, you are participating in healthy intentions and a healthy marriage as an encourager.

Marriage Struggles with Criticism: What to Do

One of the best things you can do is to take your spouse by the hand and ask him or her if they could go with you on a walk around the house. Take a piece of paper with you, go from room to room, and ask this question: "For you, Honey, what would you like to change in this room? What do you like or dislike about each room? I also would like for us to go to the garage and around the house and look at our landscape and discuss what needs to be changed." Ask him or her to give their opinion overall about the house.

Next say this: "Honey, I sense that you are unhappy with our house. I know you like to give your thoughts and ideas about what needs to change around here. So after we walked around our house, I have made a long list of house improvements we can do for the future. But I also sense you will not be happy until then. My observation about you is that your happiness depends upon something changing. I have noticed you will be happy when, or if, someday something gets done. But I don't feel you are happy now. I don't say this to be critical, but I sense your happiness gets delayed until this or that gets done.

"But to get this list done, it make take five more years. Are you going to be unhappy until then? Is your mood dependent upon these house changes? I don't want us to wait for all these changes to get done in order for us to be happy, and I especially don't want you to remain unhappy."

"Instead of us looking for things to change, how can we both find a way to encourage one another now? You tend to criticize and complain about our house, our kids, and me, and I don't feel you are happy. I would rather both of us find a way to be happy now and not delay our happiness because we need to wait to complete this list we have created. Can we find a way to be patient with the process of making these changes around this house, and instead be encouragers to one another?"

It has been my experience that critical people are unhappy people. They can be happy, but their happiness is dependent upon when or if something gets done. Instead of living in the moment, they tend to live into the future, grumbling about what is not being done. Their happiness is always delayed.

So share, in a gentle and kind way, what you notice about your spouse's mood and how it is dependent upon this or that. Communicate how you want both of you to be encouragers and be happy now, instead of waiting for happiness in the future.

Marriage Struggles with Encouragement: What to Do

After reading this chapter, and recognizing ways in which you or your spouse tend to be a critic more than an encourager, I suggest you purchase some index cards. Each morning take five minutes and create an "Encouragement Card." At the top of the card, write out this title and then think of something you are thankful for.

You see, to be an encourager means you want to be grateful and thankful. When you are grateful and thankful, you are trying to point out aspects of your spouse and your marriage that you are thankful for. Write on the index card some trait about your spouse in which you are thankful and grateful. For example, the various chores or activities he or she does around the house, or the way your spouse treats you and communicates to you.

Use a different index card each day. Write "Encouragement Card" at the top and put it somewhere your spouse will see it. Be honest, be sincere, and be positive about being thankful and grateful. Try to recognize not only the big things but also the little things as a way for you to be an encourager.

As you do this, observe what your spouse does and see if he or she makes any comments about this. Look for ways to have a conversation. Do not wait for him or her to affirm what you have written.

Instead just keep writing each day, and allow your spouse to notice and make comments about it so that the two of you are participating in building a healthy marriage. If he or she says nothing, keep writing because you want to be an encourager.

DO YOU WANT TO BE RESENTFUL OR DO YOU WANT TO BE FORGIVING?

Pre-chapter Quiz: Answer each statement either true or false as it pertains to you.

1. I tend to hide my angry feelings or thoughts from my spouse and say I am fine.

2. When we argue, I tend to give in just to avoid a fight.

3. When I get angry, I try to control it, but usually I can't and remain angry.

4. My spouse complains that I am distant and does not show affection.

5. I want my spouse to show me love and attention but usually feel disappointed.

6. I don't like to be alone, but I also feel lonely and resentful when my spouse is around.

7. My spouse and I regularly forgive one another when we make mistakes.

8. I do wish we could apologize and forgive one another and not remain mad at each other.

In your marriage, how do you view resentment? What comes to mind when you think of this word? Can you look back over your marriage and notice resentment happening either on your part or on your spouse's part, and how did that affect the marriage. Can you remember a time in your marriage when resentment got resolved and the two of you chose to forgive? The goal of this chapter is to recognize how toxic and painful resentment is to the marriage. When spouses hold onto grudges, allowing hurt to turn into anger, and this hurt and anger does not get resolved or validated by your spouse, then resentment enters the marriage.

UNHEALTHY INTENTION: FOCUS ON RESENTMENT

In general, resentment is frozen anger. Resentment is a hard, cold anger toward your spouse in response to how they treated you. When our spouse hurts us, and we do not share our hurt and this hurt does not get resolved, the hurt turns to anger. Anger is a feeling informing you that something is wrong. It is similar to a flashing signal on a car dashboard telling the driver something is wrong and the car needs some attention. I don't know about you, but when a dashboard light on my car goes off, I want to attend to it as quickly as possible. When you feel that emotion called anger, you also need to attend to it right away.

Anger is like a weed in a garden. You have a beautiful flower garden, and you notice some weeds are starting to grow and are threatening to take over your flowers. You tell yourself it would be a good idea to get rid of the weeds to prevent them from interfering with your flower garden. Weeds distract you from focusing on the flowers. But then life gets busy, your schedule brings demands and pressures, and while you feel weeding is important, you can't find the time.

In a few weeks these small weeds start to grow and multiply. They begin taking over the flower garden, choking out the flowers. The same can be true of resentment. We all struggle to let go of resentment, which is like a deeply rooted weed that spreads when we neglect attending to our hurt and anger. We start to feel and conclude that we will never be able to resolve our resentments. As a result, our unresolved, frozen anger grows quickly and deeply in our hearts, in our minds, and trust starts to break down. Resentment crowds out other feelings and destroys our happiness and trust. Unchecked, resentment can turn us into bitter and isolated people.

If you feel some anger towards your spouse and you know how important it would be to confront and talk about this anger but you don't, you then are stuffing your anger. Just like cornbread gets stuffed into the inner cavity of the turkey, likewise your hurt, anger, and mistrust can also get stuffed into the inner cavity of your heart, mind, and attitude. Anger turns into resentment when we stuff it and don't resolve it. As a result, resentment builds bitterness, hate, indifference, and annoyance with your spouse which results in feeling numb and building a wall around your heart. Then you start to think of strategies to avoid your spouse because you feel so much anger and resentment towards them. And when resentment goes deep, trust and intimacy go out the window, and you find yourself not wanting to be with your spouse. This only leads to avoiding or isolating yourself from that person.

Resentments grow out of a belief that you have repeatedly been hurt or wronged in some way. An injury has occurred in the relationship. Like a pulled muscle or a turned ankle, pain flares up, telling you something is wrong. When we fail to get treatment for body aches, the pain will last much longer, and the injury may not heal. When we fail to address a relationship injury, resentment starts to creep in. Unfortunately, as the resentment grows, we become hardened people with hard hearts and hostile attitudes towards our spouse.

In general, resentments grow and start to build due to three things: 1) intentional actions that you think of as mean or thoughtless; 2) unintentional neglect or missed opportunities; and 3) intentional neglect (what your spouse could do but seems not to want to do).

Consider the marriage of Rick and Sally. Early in their relationship, Rick tended to not want to rock the boat, as Rick was a pleaser, and Sally was an avoider. Rick liked Sally a lot and quickly wanted to spend time with her and be with her. He pursued Sally. Sally liked this pursuit and attention, and she enjoyed the laughter and the long conversations the two of them were having. Their dating became more serious, and they got engaged and then married. Sally was excited to be with Rick and was looking forward to a lifetime of being married to him. But at the same time, she also found herself getting worried about his anger.

After they got married and moved into an apartment, Sally noticed the arguments and anger increase. Sally liked and valued a clean kitchen. Rick tended to not value or participate at the same level of cleanliness that Sally aspired to. Sally found herself often asking Rick to place his dirty dishes in the dishwater, or at the very least to wash off his plate before putting it in the sink. The first few times Rick did not do this, Sally ignored it, telling herself it was not a big deal. Besides, Rick worked hard and seemed to be getting more and more stressed due to the long hours he was putting in. Sally continues to rationalize, thinking maybe Rick was just not into a clean kitchen, and maybe she was making a mountain out of a mole hill. She minimized her feelings and her irritation with him for not participating with her in keeping a clean kitchen.

But now months have gone by, and Rick's habits are hurting Sally. A good reaction would be for Sally to kindly tell Rick how her feelings are being hurt and ask if they can come up with a solution. Instead, Sally says nothing and begins to think Rick is not only neglecting the dishes but also intentionally neglecting her request, which she feels is mean and defiant. Sally stuffs her feelings, building mistrust, and starts to hold a grudge or resentment towards Rick.

Sally now does not know what to do. She has expressed anger with Rick, asked him to participate in what she wants, and feels he is intentionally doing this as a way to get back at her for complaining about the dishes. Sally starts to doubt if Rick even cares about her or the marriage anymore. Because she is feeling resentment about the dishes, she begins to make a list in her head of other things he is not doing. She thinks back to their dating relationship and how much he seemed to be in to her, wanting to help and please her. At first Rick seemed to be the type of guy she could talk and share herself with, and she felt they were a team. But now he seems a million miles away with his own thoughts and own choices, and she feels alone and abandoned. Deep down, Sally feels like they are more like roommates than husband and wife.

Now step back and look at your marriage. Are there times you did not say something when you could have? Has resentment affected your feelings towards your spouse? Your spouse is going to hurt you, intentionally or not, and it is your job to find a way to confront in love for the sake of sharing your hurt and anger so it does not turn into resentment.

Ultimately, resentment hurts us more than it hurts the other person. Peace of mind and hopeful attitudes about the other person gets minimized as we spend our time thinking about how terrible someone is or how we've been hurt. We then become stuck in the past and form very hurtful beliefs about our spouse. Resentment is about past hurts, but it poisons our present and future. It leads to difficulty with forgiveness. Sally could confront Rick about how she feels, but she now feels it's his job to address it. Sally feels he needs to take responsibility and ask how she is doing. She thinks to herself, "Why doesn't Rick care about me? Can't he see how hurt and quiet I am?"

Sally feels Rick owes her something and needs to demonstrate remorse, correct his behavior, and do the dishes in order to pay her back. Sally does not feel she did anything wrong, so she waits for Rick to make the first move, and now they are at a standstill. This idea of debt really only affects Sally. Rick does not feel he has to do something, nor is he bothered that the dishes are not being done, and he seems not to notice any unresolved anger or resentment Sally has towards him. And that is the cancer of resentment. Sally's resentment only hurts her. She is not happy, she has neglected her health and is experiencing headaches, stomach aches, weight gain, and difficulty sleeping.

This is why this topic of resentment versus forgiveness is so important in marriage. When spouses hold on to resentments, they bring the past into the present and carry it into the future. Our past resentments fuel our thinking and behavior like luggage that weighs us down. When we feel wronged, it is easy to wait for our spouse to initiate. Due to her feelings of resentment towards Rick, she is too proud to approach him and talk to him about how he hurt her. So instead she waits for him to take the initiative. Sally does not feel she did anything wrong so to make it right, Rick needs to make the first move and now they remain stuck. Resentments destroy a marriage.

HEALTHY INTENTION: FOCUS ON FORGIVENESS

The intention of resentment or forgiveness can make or break a marriage. When spouses don't talk about their hurts and find a way to resolve them, hurts turn into anger and resentment. But when spouses choose to forgive, they begin the process of healing. Resentments keep us stuck and frozen; forgiveness helps us get unstuck and unfrozen. Resentments cause us to put on masks and say we are fine; forgiveness results in us taking off our masks and being real about our hurt so we can forgive. Resentments hurt us; forgiveness heals us.

The most important aspect of forgiveness is to get to the place where you decide to forgive, to cancel the debt you feel your spouse owes you. When hurts do not get resolved in the present moment, then hurts can turn into debt expecting our spouse to make up this debt and apologize. Healthy spouses have honest conversations about hurt, not to settle the score, but to clear the air and forgive. Healthy spouses want resentment out of their marriage and want to practice apologizing and forgiveness. Healthy spouses want to keep their debt list short. Unhealthy spouses want to keep this debt list and pull out their list to use as a weapon when they are fighting.

Reconciliation happens when both spouses choose to end resentment and both spouses choose to forgive. When one spouse forgives their spouse, it helps the forgiver at least as much as the offender. It's important to remember that you can't make your spouse apologize or stop hurting you. I promise you this: even after you ask your spouse to try not to hurt you in the future, they will let you down. Spouses are going to be repeat offenders, and they will hurt you in the present and the future, regardless of whether the hurt is intentional or not. Forgiveness confronts the hurt and finds a way to forgive and let it go.

The main thing is for each spouse to answer this question: How important is it for me to value apologizing and forgiving in this marriage? It is so healthy for couples to spend time talking about how they will practice resolving hurts, forgiving one another, and letting go of resentment. This means each person must answer this question: Do I want to resent, or do I want to forgive? Forgiveness means being vulnerable and sharing your hurts in the moment with one another. If one spouse is hurt, both spouses are going to be hurting. Both people need to value the "we" and not "me" and have honest talks about resolving hurts together.

It's easy to hang on to a list of hurts, which may help you feel better about your own mistakes, or justified in pushing away from your spouse. It's easy to assume your spouse can read your mind while you stuff your feelings, waiting for your spouse to make the first move. But healthy spouses focus on addressing hurts and letting them go. Healthy spouses want trust and love and do not keep a record of wrongs.

To move from resentment to forgiveness starts with an invitation for honest conversation and vulnerability. This is the moment when Sally can approach Rick, the first few weeks after he does not wash his dirty dishes, and ask him: "Rick, do you have some time Saturday morning? I would like to talk to you about something really important to me." In this time, Sally can talk to Rick about the problem, dishes in the sink, and how she feels hurt. It is not appropriate for Sally to blast and blame Rick, or use this as an arena to express her hurts and resentment by telling him what a bad husband he is. Sally needs to talk to Rick about the problem without attacking Rick as a person. If your agenda is to fix your spouse and to get him or her to change and not hurt you, good luck. Remember the chapter on accepting versus correcting? Healthy confrontation is not an excuse to slip into unhealthy correcting behavior. When confronting your spouse, it's important to maintain acceptance and have an intention of healing, not of "getting even."

Sally could say something like this: "Resentment has entered into our marriage, and for me, resentment is not what I want. I feel undervalued and ignored when I have to do all the household chores and I am hoping we can work together and have a better understanding of resolving problems so that resentment does not poison or sabotage our marriage. This is really painful for me. It feels like you don't care. Deep down, I think you really do care, and that's why I want to talk to you. And I care too. I want to forgive past hurts and move on. Can we pursue apologizing and forgiving one another for our marriage? I think if we could find a way to resolve our hurts and differences, maybe we could negotiate to solve problems sooner. In addition, I want us to work together to solve how chores get done so we are a team doing this together. I know no plan will be perfect, and I accept that this is not a high priority for you, but I would like you to meet me partway—it would make me feel so appreciated and loved! I know I can't make you want to do this, but I am inviting you to think about it, so that resentment has no place in our marriage."

What I recommend is to write down what you plan to say on a piece of paper or an index card, or type up a letter to your spouse, ask them for some time, and read the letter out loud. Your goal is not to blindside your spouse with hurtful or angry accusations but to have this conversation in a healthy way, delivering your words in a calm and confident tone. It may help to practice reading the letter out loud to yourself in the mirror, or to a trusted friend or family member.

Healthy spouses with healthy intentions have regular conversations sharing their anger and hurt in order to forgive and let go of any resentment baggage, and move forward. When you can quickly attend to your garden and pick out the

weeds before they get too big, it will take only
an hour or so. But if you wait, you will not have
to spend all weekend pulling weeds. The same
is true for marriage. If you pull weeds, you'll
get dirty in the process. You may get blisters or
thorns in your hands—but it's worth it when you
see what the garden produces. The painful process of confronting and forgiving your spouse is
the same way. It's an uncomfortable conversation, and you'll have to swallow your pride and
be open to hearing some tough things. Think of it
as weeding the garden of your marriage. Get rid
of the resentment and focus on the fruit you can
nurture by choosing forgiveness, intimacy, closeness, empathy, kindness, respect, consideration,
and words of encouragement.

So pursue and value forgiveness over resentment. Get rid of the weeds of hurt and anger quickly. Tell your spouse about your feelings, and be
open to hearing from them as well. Let go of the
hurt and anger and pursue love and forgiveness.

Marriage Struggles with Resentment: What to Do

After reading this chapter, if you sense resentment
between you and your spouse, let me give you a
suggestion of what to do. If you are ready to put
an end to holding onto resentment, then it would
be wise to start doing this as quickly as you can.
As you know, resentment has to do with the past.
When you think back, do you remember hurtful
words or bad experiences that the two of you had
but never resolved?

My suggestion would be this: Sit down with a piece of paper and take some time to write down the patterns you notice of how the two of you have resentments towards each other. For example, maybe it has to do with your spouse failing to call to inform you what time he or she is going to be home. Not communicating will destroy trust. Mistrust and resentments happen when you don't call your spouse to inform where you are. Now that you are married, it is normal with today's smart phones to call or text what time you will be home, every day, out of respect for your spouse.

Next, write how you are resentful towards your spouse for this pattern. Write down how this pattern has hurt you and the marriage, and write down that this pattern cannot continue. Then say this to your spouse: "Honey, I am sorry to report this to you, but we have a problem. And it is something we both do, and it does hurt and affect both of us. I don't want us to be resentful into the future. I don't want this pattern to continue. I am not bringing this up because I want to micromanage or control you or tell you what you need to stop doing. Instead, I am bringing this up because this has become a pattern where we both have resentment. I want us to talk about this pattern so we can put an end to this.

"How do you feel about this pattern? Is there anything I can do to assure you I am not out to control or micromanage you? That is not my intention! Instead, I want us to work together to end this pattern, find a way to never go back and continue doing this." Try to say this with kindness and understanding that your intention is not to point out each other's mistakes. Ask your spouse if there is any pattern he or she would want for the two of you to correct and do differently in the future.

Marriage Struggles with Forgiveness: What to Do

Now that you have read this chapter and you do want to end resentments and focus on becoming a forgiving person, it would be a good idea to start to look for ways to forgive one another. As a way to do this, let me give you a suggestion.

I don't know how familiar you are with twelve step programs, but they are twelve steps for people who have habits or addictions that are hurting not only themselves but also others around them. The first step is all about admitting. Consider this step: "Hi, my name is _____, and I admit that I am powerless over _____, and my life has become unmanageable." The first step is about coming out from denial and moving to a place of admitting you are powerless over some habit or addition and how your life is unmanageable.

The goal and intention right at the start with step one is to find a way to be honest with yourself and admit you have a problem. Admitting and confessing is a good thing to do for our lives.

In the same way, learning to admit and confess to your spouse what you have done wrong and admit how your actions, choices, words, and behavior have hurt and affected the marriage is a good thing. So what you can do is this: Once a week, sit down with your spouse and admit how you have hurt them in your actions, words, choices, or behaviors, and take ownership for what you did this last week by apologizing. Make it a weekly pattern to be sincere and admit any hurts you have contributed to this marriage. Say with sadness how you have made a mistake again. Share how remorseful you feel for your choices, words, or actions, and be apologetic and confess it is your goal is to stop doing this. Then ask your spouse to forgive you. Each week, value apologizing and forgiving one another. Confession does bring healing to the marriage.

CHAPTER 8
DIFFERENCE #6

DO YOU WANT TO PURSUE JUSTICE OR DO YOU WANT TO PURSUE MERCY?

Pre-chapter Quiz: Answer each statement either true or false as it pertains to you.

1. When I get angry, I tend to pull away despite my spouse pursuing me.

2. I feel little and minimized when my spouse says mean things to me.

3. I feel my spouse and I disrespect each other and don't listen or value each other's words.

4. My spouse judges or disapproves of my choices.

5. We both tend to exhaust each other with interrogation and constant questions.

6. I tend to use negative labels, accusing my spouse or calling him or her stupid.

7. I try to show kindness and mercy to my spouse even when they don't deserve it.

8. I am tired of us punishing each other and want us to show acts of kindness instead.

When problems or conflicts happen in your marriage, do you pursue justice to address these issues, or do you pursue mercy or grace? Pursuing justice involves looking at the problem through the lens of truth, law, right, and wrong. But spouses who view marriage problems through the lens of mercy desire to be kind and caring to one another as they resolve problems.

UNHEALTHY INTENTION: FOCUS ON JUSTICE

Justice says, "An eye for an eye, and tooth for a tooth." Justice wants to keep score. Justice wants someone to pay. When justice is pursued in marriage, one or both spouses seek rules, laws, or standards to be kept and obeyed. When a spouse fails, your justice spouse might withhold trust and closeness until justice is served and punishment has been applied.

In sports competition, when two teams play against each other, someone is hired to act as judge, making sure rules and standards are followed. If an infraction occurred, the judge blows a whistle, throws a flag, and issues a penalty. Making sure athletes and sport teams follow the rules is the job of the referee. We pay police and highway patrol officers to enforce the law, and we expect these officers to uphold the law to make sure our cities and highways are safe.

So how does it feel if your spouse blows a whistle, throws a flag, and accuses you of breaking some marriage standard, judging and prosecuting you

117

Do You Want To Pursue Justice Or Do You Want To Pursue Mercy?

when you have done something wrong? Spouses who pursue justice are people who pursue the truth and want wrong to be made right. When justice and judging enters the marriage, mistrust and suspicions also enter the marriage. One spouse will start to observe and keep a record in their head of what you do to make sure there is some semblance of punishment.

Now I don't know about you, but I do not like to be judged. When you judge, you are quick to point out a fault has occurred due to them not measuring up to some standard. For spouses who judge, it is about justice needing to be applied to create fairness and balance out the scales of right and wrong. Judging says you fail to live up to some standard I have for you, and I will sit in the judge's seat to judge you.

A recent popular song sung by "Orianthi" titled "According To You[3]" summarizes feelings of being judged. A boyfriend judges his girlfriend, and she recounts in the song what she hears him saying: "According to you, I'm stupid, I'm useless, I can't do anything right. I'm difficult, hard to please, forever changing my mind. According to you, I'm boring, I'm moody, and you can't take me any place." She then contrasts this judging boyfriend and his accusations with a new boyfriend who shows mercy and kindness, and she says this about his description of her: "But according to him, I'm beautiful, incredible, he can't get me out of his head. I'm funny, irresistible, everything he ever wanted. I need to feel appreciated, like I am not hated. Why can't you see me through his eyes?" Her plea and prayer is to get her old boyfriend to see how in his judging, he has hurt her, and now she feels loved and accepted by her new boyfriend.

Think back to the chapter on correcting versus accepting. Pursuing justice looks a lot like correcting, but it adds conditions. A spouse pursuing justice would not only expect an apology, but also feel certain conditions need to be applied to make their spouse pay for their wrongs. Demanding justice gets in the way of real forgiveness and can easily lead to resentment if the one judging feels the other has not fully made amends. In other words, the justice spouse feels an apology is not good enough and they are saying to their spouse, 'yeah but.' This 'yeah but' is applying justice and conditions to the apology and will only forgive when they feel that person has lived up to the measurement or standards. An apology is one thing, amends is another thing, but justice says you have to continue to pay for how you hurt me based upon my justice system, and I get to make the call when I feel you have paid your debt to me.

Consider the marriage of Mike and Ann. They have been married for ten years and have two small children. Mike always felt a little left out, as his wife graduated from college, got a job with a large corporation, and climbed the ladder of success. He was feeling jealous that she was making more money than him, and he felt like he was less important than her career. One day he looked at

119

Do You Want To Pursue Justice Or Do You Want To Pursue Mercy?

her smartphone and found texts and pictures that shocked him—Ann was emotionally cheating on him. Mike found the man Ann had been texting, went to his job, yelled at him, shoving him and then he left. Mike felt justice had to be served by this man getting hurt for what he did to their marriage. Mike may have felt better temporarily, but no healing actually happened between him and Ann—when he goes back home, there will still be distance even if she never contacts the other man again. Perhaps Mike will demand a payment from her as well.

Problems such as cheating, stealing, lying, disrespect, drugs, alcohol, and pornography are big issues for a marriage to overcome. When one spouse intentionally does one of these things, deep hurt, mistrust, and pain will really cause one spouse to feel some sort of consequence needs to be in place in order to rebuild the relationship. But a consequence must be used to help repair the trust that has been broken. A consequence cannot be used to make your spouse suffer. The problem with using justice to solve big issues is that no consequence will make the wrongs disappear. Nothing Ann can do will erase the horrible feeling Mike felt in his gut as he looked at her phone. But perhaps if she feels remorseful and wants to repair things with Mike, they can. When spouses intentionally are out to hurt their spouse by cheating, lying, drinking or pornography, trust is broken, and the process of repairing this trust must occur.

Ann will need to do some reflecting, which

could include counseling, and a group of people holding her accountable. She will need to show Mike that she can be trusted again. Maybe Ann will have to stop going to some events she enjoys because the man she was texting with will be there. Maybe she'll have to give up her smartphone. Note that these "consequences" are not designed to make Ann suffer, though they may be difficult for her. They are designed to rebuild her marriage, so they are actually meant to help her. There is also no illusion that anything can undo what's been done—the focus is on healing and moving forward.

When a serious hurt occurs in marriage, it cannot just be ignored, or atoned for with flowers or arbitrary punishments. The couple will need to spend time in counseling talking about the issue so as to share their pain and remorse and make a plan for rebuilding their relationship. When someone hurts you, it bothers and bugs you. The question is this: does it bother and bug them? If a spouse who has made a serious mistake really does feel some remorse, has a guilty conscious, and really does want to make a change, this can happen. But it will take time depending upon the severity of the infraction. It is one thing when you forget to pay a bill; it is another thing when you cheat with your spouse's best friend. Healthy remorse and rebuilding trust are wise and good.

A lens of justice not only requires consequences to be paid for hurts; it can place conditions on love and trust. Conditions say this: "I will love you if you do this and not that." But the problem is that love

121

Do You Want To Pursue Justice Or Do You Want To Pursue Mercy?

cannot be conditional. Love has to be a choice, and love has to be free. Trust can be conditional when it has been broken as in the example above. But trust should not be conditional based on mistakes, misunderstandings, or simple differences.

For example, let's say your wife Liz goes to the movie with her friend Gail and her husband Jay feels hurt as he feels left out. It would be wrong for Jay to place conditions on Liz seeking justice. Liz went to the movies because that is what she does; she did not do this intentionally to hurt Jay. They may have different priorities or lifestyles, and this is a good place for a healthy conversation, but it is not appropriate for Jay to stop speaking to Lizzie or refuse to help her clean the bathroom (her least favorite chore) for a month.

At the root of conditions and justice is this attitude: What is in it for me? Spouses who intentionally place conditions on their spouse are wanting to see and experience evidence that not only do you apologize but also that you fulfill my conditions since love has to be earned. Justice is all about me and not our marriage and I demand justice from you. What can you do for me to meet what I expect? So then, you are responsible to fix or help cure my hurt by performing or doing certain things as conditions that I expect from you. Justice is about performing, pleasing, punishing, earning, and expecting the other person to meet conditions.

In the movie "Walk the Line" about the life of Johnny Cash, Johnny's first wife places many conditions and rules on him so that he feels he has to walk the line in order to earn her favor. As a result, he acts out in order to feel freedom when he is away from her. He does what he wants to do in rebellion against his wife, who judges him and places conditions on him when he is home.

Justice can also be a way for insecure people to build themselves up. A justice attitude places one spouse in a one up position and the other in a one down position. Justice says, "I can judge you, and I feel like I am above you and would never do what you did, therefore I am good, you are bad, and your bad behavior needs to be punished." Justice is about performing, pleasing, earning, and expecting the other person to meet conditions. It is back to the "me" attitude discussed in the first difference.

HEALTHY INTENTIONS: FOCUS ON MERCY

In general, mercy can be described as being compassionate, showing empathy, giving forbearance to an offender, and pardoning someone by showing acts of kindness. To show mercy is to say, "I may have been wronged or feel like you owe me, but I am cancelling all debts."

There are many great movies that come to mind when it comes to showing acts of mercy. A few years ago, a movie adaptation of the musical Les Miserables[4] was released, based on Victor Hugo's novel. The story can be summed up as a battle

123

Do You Want To Pursue Justice Or Do You Want To Pursue Mercy?

between justice and mercy. Javert, a policeman, lives according to truth, the law, justice, and rules. Jean Valjean lives his life according to mercy.

Jean Valjean does not have a perfect past. He was imprisoned for stealing a loaf of bread for his sick sister and her son, and his penalty for stealing was five years in prison and an additional fourteen years for numerous attempts to escape. It was a crime of kindness, but the harsh prison system and an extended sentence turn Valjean hateful and bitter. When he is finally released on parole, he attempts to survive but cannot find a job because of his past. A priest shows him mercy by giving him food and shelter in his own home, asking for no explanation or compensation. Still in survival mode, Valjean steals the priest's silverware and runs off in the night. When the police catch him and bring him back, the priest shows a rare level of mercy: he tells the police that he gave the silverware to Valjean, as well as two silver candlesticks which he had forgotten to take. Jean Valjean is left perplexed and overwhelmed by this merciful priest. As a result, he turns his life around, showing mercy as it was shown to him.

He reinvents his identity but is still on the run from the police, especially Javert, since he has broken parole. Javert is convinced Jean Valjean can never change and will always be a criminal who deserves to be punished. No mercy, no kindness. But when Valjean saves his life, Javert has a major emotional crisis. He believes in good things, in protecting people and fighting evil. Yet mercy painfully reveals the holes in his justice-only approach.

This movie has a theme of the battle between good and bad, justice and mercy. But as you know, this theme is not only played out in the movies but also in real lives every day in real homes and real marriages. We all face the challenge of what to pursue when someone hurts us: justice or mercy. Justice demands conditions and performance; mercy invites kindness and freedom.

To be a merciful spouse is to value freedom to make mistakes in your marriage and as a person. So when a spouse gets a dent in the car, a merciful response is, "Well, now that car has more character. And no one will want to steal it! Don't worry about the car; I'm so glad you're ok!" Mercy is unconditional love. Mercy says let's find new ways to accept one another rather than placing demands on one another.

To show mercy is to accept mistakes, to accept that all spouses are broken and imperfect and we all do wrong, but we choose to respond with kindness and compassion rather than with punishment. Mercy creates a safe and trusting relationship. When hurts happen, merciful spouses can talk about them after any heated emotions have cooled down but before resentment builds. Practice saying, "I am sorry I hurt you, can you forgive me?" and, "That really hurt, but I want to forgive you and move forward." Mercy seeks acceptance, justice seeks judgment.

We all need mercy to accept one another, to understand and show kindness, and to let go of the need for perfection and correction. All spouses and marriages need mercy and we all need to

125

Do You Want To Pursue Justice Or Do You Want To Pursue Mercy?

get past judging and punishing. Be a spouse that builds the marriage choosing mercy, kindness, and acceptance. Be a difference maker.

So a merciful spouse may say, "Ouch, it hurts that you are working all the time, and I feel like I never see you. How did it get to this point? How are we going to heal this broken action in our relationship?" Mercy says, "We have a problem, let's talk about this so we can figure out what damage has happened and how to repair it." Mercy says, "Welcome to the club of making mistakes. Because we are human, we are going to hurt each other, and I had better get my head around this reality." If you want to start practicing mercy, it's helpful to think of times you've made mistakes. Is there a time you messed up and someone showed you mercy? How did it feel? Try to keep this memory close at hand so that the next time your spouse makes a mistake, you will recall it and want to do the same for them. It really is something you can practice. Start with small things, and over time, the bigger things will become easier.

Marriage Struggles with Justice: What to Do

If you notice justice happening in your marriage, here are some things that you can do to stop this pattern. As you know, spouses who focus on justice are like a judge or referee. So how do you approach someone who likes to judge?

Try this: purchase a referee football jersey along with a whistle and a flag. Ask your spouse to wear this when he or she gets home from work each day or wear it this upcoming weekend. Tell your spouse you are giving them permission to judge you. When they notice you have made a mistake and you need to be punished, ask them to throw the flag and blow the whistle. Remind them since there is judging going on in this marriage, you want him or her to wear the uniform as a way to reinforce judging and justice. Obviously, I would not recommend this strategy if you are in a physical abusive marriage.

As you know, your spouse probably will not go along with this idea. They may get hurt, or they may laugh and may not care at all. My experience with spouses who judge is that they do not want to be mocked or made fun of. But you need to be serious about how you experience your spouse being out to judge you. Share with him or her that if the shoe fits, than he or she might as well wear it.

The goal is to shake him or her up to help them focus on the reality of judging and justice being done in this marriage. Share how hurt and serious you are about wanting to stop punishing and judging one another.

For example, a big problem with judging in marriages usually involves money. Let's say your spouse is judging you for the way you spend money. Ask your spouse to put on the uniform, as that is how you feel being judged for your spending habits. Inform them that you do not want to pay for your choices. Remind your spouse if she or he wants to judge, they can, but then that means

127

Do You Want To Pursue Justice Or Do You Want To Pursue Mercy?

you can go out and buy more of what you do not need. Be prepared for fairness to happen as your spouse may do tit for tat. Allow this to happen for a month. Spend money just to prove your point. My hope is, both of you will eventually say no more, surrender, and make a commitment to not spend money outside the budget unless you both are in agreement. Better yet, give up judging and justice in your marriage completely.

Marriage Struggles with Mercy: What to Do

When you want mercy in your marriage, then you are ready to bring kindness into the marriage. When you are merciful, it is expressed through acts of kindness to show your love for one another.

How do you do this? Sit down with a piece of paper and write down all the things you can do for your spouse above and beyond what you normally do. Consider what makes him or her happy. Try to think of their favorite food and cook it once a week. Get up early and wash the car before your spouse goes to work one morning. The goal is to brainstorm ways to show acts of kindness and mercy towards your spouse.

The best time to do this is when he or she does not deserve it. Maybe the two of you got into a fight the day before, or maybe your spouse made a huge mistake and you are mad and hurt by what he or she did. Sure, take a few days to process this, but as quickly as you can, take the initiative and show mercy as a way to forbid hurt and judging in your marriage. Say to your spouse you could remain angry and punish him or her with silence for a few days. But instead you are trying to do something different to bring healing, expressing acts of kindness and mercy. Always remember this, mercy says you do not deserve it, but because I love you, I want to show you mercy rather than judging you.

DO YOU WANT TO AVOID CONVERSATION OR DO YOU WANT TO CLARIFY CONVERSATION?

Pre-chapter Quiz: Answer each statement either true or false as it pertains to you.

1. I avoid conflict with my spouse by being dishonest in my communication.

2. When my spouse is mad at me, I try to do something nice to gain their approval.

3. When my spouse wants to go out to eat, I usually defer to their choice for the restaurant.

4. I tend to pursue my spouse for connection more so than my spouse pursues me.

5. I seek ways to keep my spouse close to me so they will not pull away from me.

6. I do my best to be patient and listen when we communicate.

7. When I am puzzled or annoyed by what my spouse says, I try to ask for clarification.

8. I wish my spouse would listen and pay attention to me when we share our ideas.

Unhealthy spouses avoid talking about marriage conflicts. Healthy spouses pursue having conversation about conflict for the sake of clarifying each spouse's intentions. When spouses avoid communicating and clarifying, they may falsely conclude that the problem will disappear. But avoiding often leads to more problems.

Unhealthy Intention: Focus on Avoiding Conversation

Can you define or recognize the strategy of avoidance? I believe all people avoid certain things or certain people in their lives. In some ways, avoiding can be healthy. A diabetic will probably want to avoid sugar, which is good. But they may also avoid taking their insulin for fear of pain, or testing their blood for fear of the result, which could be very dangerous. This chapter is about avoiding versus having conversations which may be painful

131

Do You Want To Avoid Conversation Or Do You Want To Clarify Conversation?

but are very important for understanding each other.

Do you strategically avoid your spouse in order to not have conversations? Let's say you get hurt and then become disillusioned about sharing your feelings with your spouse. To avoid having conversation is to falsely think your hurt emotions will go away without you having to discuss them. To avoid is to wish and fantasize marriage conflicts will go away, get swept underneath the carpet and given enough time, problems will fade away and you won't have to face it. Maybe you tell yourself not to make a mountain out of a molehill, or to make peace and not conflict, and conclude it won't do any good to talk about problems. But this is not living in reality.

Perhaps you think marriage should not have conflict. You want to pursue a love relationship and maybe you think that means never saying anything that could lead to conflict. Or perhaps you feel independent and self-sufficient and conclude you do not need anything from your spouse, and therefore, you have no desire to talk about problems. Becoming a lone ranger is the mantra of spouses who avoid. You may feel like you should be able to solve problems and get over hurts on your own without causing your spouse any stress. If you have a memory bank filled with hurtful conversations, arguments and fights, it may take time and effort for you to build up trust and feel safe approaching your spouse. You also may be waiting and predicting an argument will happen again, and you want to lessen the frequency of talking about marriage problems. Spouses who avoid have no trust nor assurance that problems can be resolved quickly or at least, without there being a fight or argument. They don't have any confidence or trust conversations can lead to resolving conflicts.

If you can identify as being a spouse who avoids, my heart goes out to you. You have far too many memories of experiencing conversations not being resolved in a healthy way. You have no confidence that conversations will not lead to an argument, fight, accusations, or blame. Maybe your spouse has a tendency to want to be right. Your experience in the past is one person is out to win their arguments and you feel like you lose every time. So you avoid to protect yourself from further pain. You say to yourself, "I would rather change the oil in the car or go into my man or woman cave and chat on Facebook or watch ESPN than talk to my spouse." Your avoidance makes sense. To have conversation for the sake of clarification and understanding means taking a risk. In general, spouses who avoid do not take risks. They want to play it safe, be comfortable, and are hesitant to take a risk. In some ways they behave like a turtle: They will stick their head out if they feel it is safe to come out, but if not, they will hide and avoid inside their thick shell.

To avoid means avoiding important conversations. It is possible that someone loves to talk to their spouse but is still avoiding important conversations. They are fine with talking about news

133

Do You Want To Avoid Conversation Or Do You Want To Clarify Conversation?

events, work, church, hobbies, sports, or projects around the house. These topics are safe. But if they feel the conversation starts to head towards talking about themselves or the marriage, they will shut down. They fear their spouse is out to criticize or blame them, so they become independent and self-sufficient, depending upon themselves, and not really feel the need to talk with their spouse. They are fearful of addressing marriage topics such as trust, feelings, hurt, or intimacy. As a result, if you ask them how they are doing, they usually say they are fine and give one to two word answers.

Spouses who avoid perceive their spouse as not a safe and trusting person. Spouses who avoid remember the conversation two weeks ago when their spouse blamed them or accused them and they perceive this will happen over and over again. Spouses who avoid have memories from their past feeling criticized, attacked, accused or blamed. So if one spouse wants to talk about household money and budget usually the avoider says fine. But when the conversation regarding money does not go well, the spouse who avoids pulls away due to the accusations or criticism told to them of how they incorrectly spend money. Their spouse pursues them trying to talk and at the same time accusing them of avoiding. Now they feel attacked, hurt, blamed and they lack any trust that conflicts about household money will get resolved in a healthy way. Poor resolution and hurtful accusations only lead to further evidence why spouses should avoid and they want to be left alone.

As a child, spouses who avoid have witnessed, watched and experienced conflict from their parents. Terri was like that. She can look back at her childhood and remember when her parents were fighting. Terri remembers her parents not just arguing but remembers the two of them engaging in physical abuse and using hurtful, angry, mean words to each other. She remembers as a 10-year old girl sitting on the couch observing her parents fighting and using hurtful and derogatory words she had never heard before. Terri also remembers when she sensed her dad was coming home, she and her sisters would run out the back door looking for ways to avoid their father at all costs. Terri studied her dad, watched and observed what type of mood he was in to determine if to avoid or not.

Deep down, spouses who avoid are highly sensitive people trying to make sure they are not going to be attacked. They also are waiting for the metaphorical shoe to drop, anticipating that anything good they have will not last.

Consider the marriage of Debbie and Larry. When they met, Debbie liked Larry, and he seemed to be kind and considerate of her and seemed to want to be there for her. Initially, they liked spending time together. Debbie liked the way Larry made her feel; he seemed to have eyes only for her. Larry liked the fact that Debbie was social and generous toward him, and he enjoyed her tendency to be dramatic and fun. She liked to talk and laugh, and he found her entertaining.

135

Do You Want To Avoid Conversation Or Do You Want To Clarify Conversation?

When Debbie and Larry met, he was unsure of what to do with his life. He decided to go back to college and get his degree in engineering and then pursued his master's degree in electric engineering. After he graduated, he asked Debbie to marry, and she said yes. Debbie was happy and excited to get married, as Larry had landed a job at an engineering firm, and she felt secure in knowing he would be working full time, and she was ready to start a family. Their first few years went well, and they fell into roles of Debbie being the caregiver and Larry being the provider.

But about five years into the marriage, Debbie started to notice a pattern that hurt her. She would approach Larry to discuss problems or issues about their children or about their marriage. He would get angry with her, asking why she would bring up topics about the kids when he was overwhelmed from work, tired, and just wanted to come home and relax. Debbie started to notice that when the kids acted up, he would grow impatient, get angry, and be irritated at Debbie for how the kids were acting up. Debbie would approach Larry to talk about her feelings and how hurt she was from Larry being critical or controlling in his parenting style. Larry would get defensive when Debbie confronted him, telling her how many hours he was working and how he was tired of coming home each night needing to help Debbie parent the children.

These arguments led to Debbie wanting to talk but fearing Larry's response. She would make sure the children had finished their chores and tell them to play quietly in their rooms as soon as Larry got home. When Larry asked her about her day, she felt free to share but was cautious not wanting to make him angry. Debbie started to notice they were growing farther apart, but she didn't know why. She wondered if she had done something wrong. She asked Larry if they could talk, and he said they could talk on Sunday. But when Debbie approached him on Sunday, he did not want to talk. Debbie pursued, he avoided, and they now were feeling more like roommates. She learned to walk on eggshells around him being careful not to get him angry. Over the years, she learned to tolerate him and avoided having conversation with Larry given he seemed to not want to talk. On one hand, she liked Larry being the strong one, the provider, the rock that she could lean on. He was a hard worker and she did respect him. Debbie missed Larry.

As a marriage and family therapist, I have witnessed this pattern of one spouse who wants to please and pursue and the other spouse who prefers to avoid and not converse. What I would say to Debbie is that she must be patient. She must make sure she is not placing conditions on Larry, putting pressure on him, or blame or get angry when he avoids her. If Larry feels the demand or pressure to talk, he will be hesitant, given he has a stored memory of conversations between the two of them in which he felt blamed and accused and this hurt has not been resolved. Spouses like Larry who

137

Do You Want To Avoid Conversation Or Do You Want To Clarify Conversation?

avoid are afraid to be vulnerable and share given they do not sense safety or trust.

The hope for Larry is to look within himself for how to be vulnerable again and try to take the risk to converse. For example, he could ask these questions of himself: "Is my avoiding approach bringing me the happiness, love, romance, and sexuality I was looking for when Debbie and I got married? I did want fun, love, happiness, and enjoyment with Debbie but now we don't have it. Is avoiding her helping my hurt feelings to heal or just hiding them?" Can Larry see he is avoiding the very thing he liked about Debbie, and avoiding the very things he was looking forward to when they got married? The challenge for Debbie and Larry is to have a conversation regarding their marriage rather than avoiding this conversation. If they do not do this, Debbie and Larry will remain lonely and drift apart concluding this is as good as it gets. Larry and Debbie are stuck. And to me, that is very sad.

HEALTHY INTENTION: FOCUS ON CLARIFYING

Spouses who pursue a marriage based upon clarifying conversations want and value an emotional connection. Spouses who value clarity want to understand the intentions of their spouse because they want love, trust, and closeness. To build a marriage based upon clarification, two things are very necessary: safety and affirmation. Spouses can communicate safety in their words and actions by demonstrating kindness, patience, understanding, and empathy. It is much easier to have clarifying conversations when both people feel safe. In a safe marriage, one does not have to fear criticism or blame. When both spouses perceive safety and trust, clarifying conversations can go much smoother.

In addition to building safety, clarifying spouses must also build affirmation. To affirm someone is to point out all the ways you value, love, respect, and believe in them and their character. To affirm is to build up the other person in words and actions of encouragement. To affirm is to encourage and accept them just the way they are. When both safety and affirmation are built into the marriage as a foundation, becoming vulnerable to clarify can happen. A false strategy for pleasers married to a spouse who avoids is to try to please, love, give, and do all sorts of things for them. But if the avoider perceives there is neither safety nor affirmation, clarifying conversations will not happen.

When you avoid, you walk in fear with anxiety. When you clarify, you walk in confidence, believing the two of you can resolve issues and problems. When you avoid, you minimize problems, sweep them under the carpet, assume as time goes by the problem will go away. When you clarify, you acknowledge hurt or conflict, and you want to resolve things so the two of you do not harbor resentment but instead resolve problems by clarifying each spouse's intention.

139

Do You Want To Avoid Conversation Or Do You Want To Clarify Conversation?

Spouses who want to clarify are not thinking about how they have been hurt, how they want to lick their wounds and pull away, or how their spouse is a horrible person. Rather, they seek and value their spouse and want to focus on conflict resolution. Spouses who avoid have been hurt and this hurt has not been resolved so they feel stuck. Being alone and fixing their hurt wounds is a much better strategy for spouses who avoid. Avoiders say I need something, you did not give it to me, and therefore I will hide and avoid and conclude you will not give it to me.

When spouses who avoid are fine with connecting as long as they feel the goal of connection is not to blame or accuse them. When confronting their avoidance, it is very important not to attack or blame, as this will lead to more avoidance. To ask a spouse who avoids, "How come you don't want to talk with me?" is to set them up for having to justify or make excuses. It also could make them feel like something is wrong with them. If your spouse is avoiding, they may recognize the importance of talking to you. But they have not had positive emotional connections or experiences, to make them feel they will be loved and accepted when they try to talk and share when it comes to marriage conflicts. This is not necessarily your fault. It is very important for your spouse to feel safe talking to you. This means you will need to listen openly, trying to see their point of view, without judging or criticizing them. If you know you tend to criticize and your spouse tends to avoid, you might try using a professional mediator or counselor to help you get started in having important conversations. That is why every marriage must have honest conversations clarifying what the marriage stands for. Do you both value and want safety, trust, respect, empathy, understanding, and affirmation of how you are going to resolve conflicts? Spouses who want to clarify are seeking not just to talk about conflicts but want to go deeper to address the foundation of the marriage-safety and affirmation. They want to pursue a deeper way of relating so when conflicts or issues come up, they first of all want to make sure the foundation of the relationship has not been hurt or destroyed. Clarifying spouses want the "we" and value the marriage; avoiding spouse's value self-protection and want to fix problems as they arise, but not necessary address the relationship.

When you get married, conflicts, hurts, misunderstandings, and relationship problems are going to happen. But when spouses value clarifying and not avoiding, I promise you, your marriage will soar above life issues, and there will be a confident attitude in the marriage that whatever does happen, we believe in us. Clarifying spouses act like a team working together so that we can clarify and understand for the sake of building a healthy marriage. So be a difference maker, seek acceptance, and find ways to pursue safety and affirmation to build healthy clarifying conversation with your spouse. And as you do this, I promise you will find a marriage and a spouse you want to come home to.

141

Do You Want To Avoid Conversation Or Do You Want To Clarify Conversation?

Marriage Struggles with Avoiding: What to Do

If you notice your spouse avoiding, you can start with asking clarifying questions such as, "How come we do not trust each other? What has happened between the two of us where you sense I am not trustworthy?" The clarifying spouse could also ask: "What have I done today or this week in which I have not built safety or affirmed you that has resulted in the two of us not feeling a level of trust? Can I do anything to help heal what I have done so we can learn to talk about the hurt rather than avoid? Can I say I am sorry, and can we get back to loving and accepting one another?"

So for Larry and Debbie, it would be healthy to ask each other whether they perceive safety and affirmation in their marriage. Do they both like and value having trust and encouragement in this marriage? How would they rate and view various values such as trust, safety, empathy, respect, and understanding happening between the two of them? Do they want to listen and solve conflicts? When Larry and Debbie can lay down the foundation of safety and affirmation, then clarifying conversations will go much more smoothly.

Spouses who want to clarify are seeking to just not talk about conflicts but want to go deeper to address the foundation of the marriage: safety and affirmation. Spouses who clarify are tired and exhausted over the arguing and fighting in the marriage. They want to pursue a deeper way of relating so when conflicts or issues come up, they first of all want to make sure the foundation and base of the relationship has not been hurt or destroyed. Clarify spouses are not trying to fix problems, nor out to confront you for the sake of wanting to attack you as being the problem. Clarifying people want the "we" and value the marriage; avoiding spouses value themselves and want to fix the problem but not necessary address the relationship.

So how do you do this? The challenge is to think of ways not to contribute to criticism and rejection. So think about last week. Think of some ways in which conversations went well, and when they did not go well. Consider the times you noticed either yourself or your spouse shutting down. Think of ways you may have contributed to your spouse avoiding, shutting down, and not wanting to talk.

Next, write your spouse a letter. Ask him or her for a few minutes and read this letter to your spouse. Communicate how sad and sorry you feel if you did anything to hurt your spouse. Be sincere that you want to apologize for how you hurt them in your words or actions.

Communicate words of empathy and understanding to your spouse. Try to get into their world of how they are feeling, and attempt to understand how they may experience feelings of being rejected or criticized. Apologize and promise you will do your best not to harm them in the future.

Look for ways to do something different next time to assure your sensitive spouse that you do not want them to avoid. Ask them what you can do to make up for the way they have been hurt. Remind them you are there for them and you do

143

Do You Want To Avoid Conversation Or Do You Want To Clarify Conversation?

believe in "us" and "our" marriage. Reassure them you do not want anyone else but him or her.

Marriage Struggles with Clarifying: What to Do

One of the main ways for your marriage to become healthy is for you to learn how to communicate with your spouse. To participate in clarifying conversation is to begin valuing clarity, communication, and understanding. Don't assume you understand anything your spouse says. Clarify and make sure you understand what they mean when they talk to you.

How do you do this? What I suggest you do is type up a communications report card. Write down various aspects of communication. For example, the first question might be: "How did I do by focusing and listening when you talked?" A second question could be, "Did I turn off any of my electronic equipment and listen to you?" A third question might be, "How did I do in responding to your text message in a timely manner?" A fourth question might be, "Did you experience me as empathetic and understanding, working with you to resolve some conflict?"

Write out these questions and any other questions you can think of and give the report card to your spouse, asking him or her to grade you on a scale of 1-5 with 1 being high and 5 being low. Ask your spouse each week to grade you on how well you listened and clarified in the past week. Then ask your spouse to also fill out this report card. Invite your spouse to join you as you both give feedback to each other on how well you two are doing in listening, clarifying, and focusing.

Share with your spouse that your intention is to find ways to clarify by asking questions for the purpose of going deeper in how you communicate. Give each other honest feedback as you both value clarifying and not avoiding conversations.

DO YOU WANT TO FOCUS ON PAST HURTS OR PRESENT HURTS?

Pre-chapter Quiz: Answer each statement either true or false as it pertains to you.

1. I get angry at my spouse when they don't affirm my hurt or ask what is wrong.

2. When my spouse hurts me, I stuff my hurt and pain and do not say anything.

3. My spouse and I are good friends and are genuinely interested in one another.

4. When I am hurt, I feel safe to share my hurt, trusting my spouse will listen.

5. I can effectively communicate my hurts and conflicts in our marriage.

6. I don't feel safe, nor do I trust my spouse to listen to my feelings.

7. I wish my spouse would not punish me, bringing up past hurts of what I have done wrong.

8. I do wish we could resolve old hurts and deal with current conflicts as a way to build trust.

This difference is about discerning the importance of how you view time in your marriage. When you got married, both you and your spouse began a journey of time together, viewing the future with excitement. As the weeks, months, and years have gone by, memories got built into the marriage. It is easy for couples to sit down and recall various events, both good and bad, of what happened to them in the past and the experiences they have had together. Some events from your past bring about pleasure, meaning, and happiness. However, other events have caused trauma or hurtful memories of what your spouse said or did, and those events can haunt and hurt your marriage.

UNHEALTHY INTENTION: FOCUS ON THE PAST

The challenge in understanding this difference is this, when a problem or crisis comes up in the present, do you and your spouse tend to focus on the past, pointing out bad memories, or do you tend to focus on the present, wanting to solve the current problem? When you approach your spouse to talk about a conflict, how quickly do you notice either yourself or your spouse returning back to memories or stories from the past and bringing them into the present argument? What is that like for you?

We each have a past. Sometimes people stay focused on hurts, anger, resentment, and memories from the past. What has happened in the past has not been resolved in their minds or hearts, and they continue to get stuck presently remembering what their spouse did to them. They may start to think about how people have disappointed them, neglected them, or been abusive with words or actions, and they find themselves thinking about this over and over again.

As you know, police detectives and crime investigators want to focus on the past to determine the people and events involved in a crime. A good detective will focus on past events like looking at a puzzle, wanting to put the pieces together so that the crime makes sense. There are many television shows, movies, and stage plays focused on crime investigation, and they include lots of exploration of the past as a way to make sense of it. In some ways this is good, in remembering the bad past for the sake of not repeating it. Many good lessons can be learned from the past.

But when it comes to marriage, how much time does a couple spend on the history, focusing on what someone did or didn't do and how this event or that event still hurts not only the spouse but also the marriage? It is one thing to have a conversation about 9-11 each year, remembering this horrible day and the fallout and tragedy of lost lives. But it is another thing in marriage to talk about what happened last year when your spouse failed you, hurt or disappointed you, and now the present is triggering old feelings and hurts that have not been resolved. A marriage gets stuck when one spouse still feels the rawness and freshness of an old wound, and both spouses need to process and heal this old wound so it does not presently affect your current marriage.

The challenge for couples is to answer this question: How much of the past, with all its baggage, are we going to be carrying with us into the future? The past can be like luggage full of old clothes which you can't wear anymore but drag around with you, weighing you down. Healthy baggage is a box full of mementos—remembering the good, loving, and happy events or experiences. Unhealthy baggage is a refusal to let go of bad events and negative experiences. This past baggage not only hurts you but also hurts the marriage.

I am all for resolving past hurts or events. If your spouse wants to talk to you about last week for the purpose of resolving a conflict, do not get defensive and justify-get empathetic and apologetic. If your spouse has an issue with you and their intention is to resolve a past event, then that is great! Hurts happen, and we need to be patient with each other, especially around sensitive issues, so that each spouse takes the proper time to talk with the other about the past as a way to resolve it. This is a healthy habit to practice.

But when spouses remain stuck in the past, this creates an unhealthy marriage. In the present when spouses are having an argument about these past hurts and events, it is like getting back on a merry-go-round, rehashing and retelling old pain over and over again. This type of response will only lead to one person getting defensive, as the other person is attacking them. The boxing gloves come on, and the fight ensues. Like a detective looking for evidence, they focus on the past, and now in the present they have done their investigation and have concluded one spouse is at fault.

In general, spouses who bring up the past have unresolved hurts and conflicts. Their past baggage has not been resolved, and they are bringing up the past in the present due to hurts, fears, doubts, and mistrust. People who bring up the past need to feel validation and closure. When we come to the realization that our past is unfinished baggage, then we can realize this baggage has not been resolved, ended, or finished. When we do not put closure to our past baggage, it will get triggered, and buttons will get pushed in the present. The more spouses can resolve to leave their baggage behind and put closure to it, the more spouses can find a way to stay in the present.

Sometimes people bring up the past as a way to prevent being dismissed, minimized, or controlled, and to ensure that what happened in the past will not get repeated in the present or future. Bringing up the past can be an attempt to feel control, bringing up points, attacks, and blame is a way people try to ensure that this time they will be heard and not rejected.

Spouses stuck in the past tend to place blame. They tend to take on a victim stance or a "poor me" stance in which they are looking for attention, sympathy, or empathy, and they are wishing this time around in the present that their spouse will give them empathy or validate how they are feeling so they can feel heard and understood which they didn't receive in the past. The stance of people bringing up the past is often this: "You hurt me in the past, you are hurting me again now, it is your fault, and it is your responsibility to fix and heal my hurt since you are the one who hurt me in the past. I am hurt, you hurt me, now you fix it, and if you don't, I am going to keep on bringing this up until you do something different."

HEALTHY INTENTION: FOCUS ON THE PRESENT

Kenny Rogers wrote a song called "Through the Years.[5]" Consider the words: "I can't remember when you weren't there, when I didn't care for anyone but you. I swear, we've been through everything there is, Can't imagine anything we've missed, Can't imagine anything the two of us can't do. Through the years, you've never let me down, you turned my life around, the sweetest days I've found, I've found have been with you. Through the years, I've never been afraid, I've loved the life we've made, and I'm so glad we've stayed, right here with you, through the years."

Hopefully, the goal of all our marriages is to repeat what Kenny Rogers sang to his wife. A marriage has many memories, both good and bad, through the years. The challenge is to create more good than bad memories so that at the end of the years together, each spouse can say, "I too am glad we have stayed together through the years."

Focusing on the present does not mean ignoring the past. It means valuing good memories and learning from bad memories, resolving them and giving them their proper place-in the past. It means acknowledging both the good and the bad and dealing with mistakes in a healthy way.

Spouses who live in the present value confession. What do I mean by that? To confess is to align yourself with the realty of saying to your spouse, "Oops, I did it again." To confess in the present is to agree and to admit: "I have hurt you, what I did irritated you, and I agree with you, my bad, I blew it, I take ownership presently for what I did to hurt you." The sooner one spouse can find a way to confess, to be vulnerable, and to be transparent, without any shame, the sooner the other spouse will recognize new patterns and not hide. And that is when honesty and transparency can emerge.

This means walking in the light and not in the darkness. Be real, be open, and honest in the present so new patterns start to emerge. Grieve the ways you have hurt each other and value quick resolution of conflict. Come out of hiding and be present, taking responsibility for how you have hurt your spouse. When one spouse feels sad, and not shamed, then healing takes place. But if one spouse feels shamed all the time and the other spouse reinforces this, shame will haunt and keep spouses stuck. Moving from self-shaming to sadness, remorse, and apology will help you build a better future. As a result, forgiveness can take place in the present.

Spouses who live in the present also resist the temptation to say, "That is just the way it is," or, "That is just the way I am." Don't give up by falsely concluding you can't change your old ways. Begin the process by choosing to change and getting rid of the hurtful baggage. Don't wait for the other spouse to do it first. It is tempting to conclude that if the other person would change their ways first, then life would be better. But waiting on someone else to change may mean waiting forever. Start with yourself, focus on the ways you contribute to living in the past, and find ways to make some changes so that each spouse wants to live in the present for a better future. Each person needs to examine their own ways and patterns. When that happens, the marriage can grow as both spouses are in the growth process of wanting to live in the present.

The fruit or benefit of living in the present is to get excited about living just one day at a time. What a difference this makes in a marriage! As a couple, set a boundary regarding past hurts and past unhealthy patterns needing to be repeated in the present and look for ways in the present to build new, healthy emotional corrective experiences. Become a spouse in the present who says, "No, we are not doing this again."

So take your spouse by the hand, sit down on the couch, and confess your faults quickly in the present moment, so old resentments and grudges do not carry on. Ask for forgiveness so you both can cancel the debt of hurt and resentment. Put an end to the ways of the past, find a way to build closure, and look for ways to really desire life to be better just for today. Put away any distractions (this includes phones and tablets) and say to your spouse, "I want thirty to sixty minutes of your focused time, and you have my undivided time and attention in order to live in the present. I want to spend time with you for the sake of not hiding or avoiding each other. I want to do things differently now to ensure a better future." As you do this and it becomes a routine each day, both spouses will begin stopping the accusations from the past and moving forward toward accepting one another now and into the future.

Marriage Struggles with Past Hurt: What to Do

When you are ready to put closure to the past, you must decide how to resolve conflict in the present so it does not become another issue you carrying around and put into your luggage bag. Spouses who want a happy marriage put closure to old hurts and wounds and find ways to protect their present so the past does not poison the present and future. Probably one of the best strategies to do this is to value learning how to hate that an old pattern of relating or communicating has emerged again.

To hate does not mean that you hate your spouse. Sure, to change old patterns will take time and spouses will make mistakes and slip back into old unhealthy habits. To hate is be frustrated that the two of you get back on the merry go round and are repeating the same old pattern. Maybe what you two can hate is to not return to blaming each other. Say to your spouse: I hate that we blame and point fingers accusing each other instead of each person taking ownership for the problem. Value finding a way to not go back to old patterns and baggage. A good exercise that I recommend to spouses is to make a list of five to ten things in your marriage that they know they never want to go back and do again. Maybe it was a time when they crossed the line and hit or pushed their spouse. Maybe it was a time when they intentionally wanted revenge and did something just to get back at the other person. We are human and do hurt each other, intentionally or not, but we all must be mature and learn from our past so we can make a turn and do something new.

I use the word "hate" as a means to motivate you to want to stop negative patterns and arguments. In other words, healthy hate is when both spouses decide to hate how you fight or go into defense mode or accusing mode in order to protect yourself from having to deal once again with past baggage that has not been resolved. Learning to hate means asking your spouse to join you in finding a way to hate hurting each other, so the two of you can really put closure to the past so that it does not poison your present and future.

When both spouses value each other and decide they never want to repeat their mistakes, both people want to build a better future. If one spouse values this but still has a hard time resolving old hurts and resentments, it might be a good idea for the couple to see a counselor so past hurtful memories can be resolved. Some past hurts, like cheating or physical, emotional, or verbal abuse may take some time. But when couples work on this together, it is like applying antibiotics to the wounds, so spouses learn, heal, and promise never to go back and do this again. In many ways, learning to hate means valuing repentance. I know this is not a word we use much today in our conversations or thinking. To repent is to make a U-turn, go in a different direction, and focus on making a change. To repent means not wanting to go back and repeat hurtful patterns or do mean things to one another.

Marriage Struggles with Present Hurt: What to Do

For your marriage, the goal is to resolve hurt and pain quickly in the moment. We know this may not happen all the time, given you may be out with friends or at an event, and it may be more challenging to resolve things in the moment. But the key is to find a way, as best you can, not to go bed angry at your spouse. That is the hope.

So what I would suggest is work together with your spouse to find some type of gesture or expression as a way to communicate when either one of you feels present hurt and pain. Maybe the gesture could be taking your hands and signaling a "time out" similar to athletes signaling to the referee for a time out. Or maybe you can agree on an inconspicuous word or phrase you can use. Your chosen gesture or word will communicate, "I need sooner rather than later some time with you to talk."

Then find a private place to share what is hurting you. Not blaming, yelling, being accusatory, or intentionally wanting to be mean. Say to your spouse, "We have a problem. I need a few minutes to share my hurt and how this hurt is affecting me but also how I feel about what you did." For example, if your spouse disrespected you, say "I don't want to go into survival mode and just take care of me because I feel hurt and disrespected. But I do want to resolve this hurt. How are we going to resolve this hurt together so we do not let this hurt ruin our day?"

I realize to do this will mean taking a risk. When trust is high, hopefully you can take this risk. It means you don't want to stuff your pain or store it up to use as ammunition in the future. Instead say to your spouse: "I do value me, and I do value you, and I do believe in us, and I want us to be a team resolving pain together. I am hurt, you're not, so what do you suggest we should do about this?"

The goal is for the two of you to find solutions resolving pain presently so this hurt gets resolved and resentment does not build up. Make sure you apologize and affirm your intention that it is not your goal to continue hurting one another. Be reminded that when trust is low, your willingness to risk and share your hurt will be low. When you are ready, communicate your hurt with the goal of the two of you presently resolving hurt and conflict.

When spouses value wanting to live in the present, both spouses want to hate and repent from repeating the same hurtful patterns over and over again. The sooner spouses can put an end to past hurts, the sooner they will start building a healthier future. Remember this: If you want to build a healthy future, you are going to need to build a healthy present. Can you look into the future and picture a healthy marriage due to the healthy work you are doing presently to create this? In other words, all healthy futures happen in all areas of life because of the healthy activities on a day by day basis.

CHAPTER 11
DIFFERENCE #9

DO YOU WANT TO PURSUE IDEAL EXPECTATIONS OR DO YOU WANT TO PURSUE REALISTIC EXPECTATIONS?

Pre-chapter Quiz: Answer each statement either true or false as it pertains to you.

1. I get angry with my spouse when they don't live up to my expectations.

2. In our first year of marriage there was passion and excitement, but now there is little love.

3. We both have interests, friends, and hobbies apart from each other.

4. I often feel I must earn my spouse's favor, trying to do something perfect.

5. I feel pressured to be like others that my spouse finds to be ideal.

6. I feel pressured to live up to my spouse's expectations and fear I may not be able to.

7. I desire for my spouse and I to find a way to accept each other for who we really are.

8. I look forward to the day when my spouse and I can live with realistic expectations.

This difference regards expectations. In your marriage, do you focus on pursuing ideal expectations or realistic expectations? Which expectation leads to peace and contentment in your marriage? When you have peace and contentment in your marriage, you are living with realistic expectations. But if spouses are pursuing idealistic expectations, peace will be replaced by stress, anxiety, and fear.

UNHEALTHY INTENTION: FOCUS ON IDEAL EXPECTATIONS

Getting married is similar to merging two companies into one. Each company has their own style and mode of operation. But when another company comes along and wants to buy or merge with them, there is always an adjustment, which can be challenging. Who will be in charge, whose approach will be followed, and what will be marketed are just a few of the issues merging companies need to resolve.

The same can be said for two people choosing to get married, merging two lives. Being single, living your own life, and living by your own expectations is very different from living with someone else and feeling their expectations, and it can be challenging. Being married is tough work, and how two

161

Do You Want To Pursue Ideal Expectations Or Do You Want To Pursue Realistic Expectations?

people, with all their differences and ways about them, learn how to merge together as husband and wife is the challenge. People every day want to get married. They value sharing life with someone to love, and they value being loved by someone. And this is all good.

But when two people get married and merge their lives together, this topic of expectation becomes very important. The reason it is important is that idealistic expectations from one spouse will put pressure and demands on the marriage. Many times, one spouse will come to realize they did not know their spouse had idealistic expectations of them or the marriage. Far too often, one spouse will have ideal expectations and set the bar high putting pressure on their spouse and their marriage, and the spouse receiving these expectations gets blindsided. When one spouse has private expectations that are not communicated during dating or engagement, this is unfair to the other spouse. And that is when marriages can get into trouble.

For example, many companies value excellence at the workplace. As an employee, to be your best, give your all, and have high standards by which you work is a good thing. Or let's say you need surgery. A good idea is to find a surgeon or hospital that values practicing excellence. If someone is going to operate on me, I want them to have high standards and pursue excellence in order to ensure this surgery is done correctly. Having high standards of excellence is a good thing, as I do not want to come back a second time to have another surgery to correct the first surgery. No one wants sloppy or haphazard efforts from a physician they are trusting with their health.

But when we ask our spouses to do love, intimacy, and communication as tasks, making sure they do it according to our ideal standards, we begin the process of demanding something from our spouse. A surgeon operates and does a task. But marriage cannot be a task. Love and intimacy cannot be a task. Being married is all about relating and being intimate with one another. When we relate, it is all about being and engaging with this person. Marriage is not a doing task, it is a relating activity. I am not looking for the surgeon to relate to me in activities such as love, intimacy, or closeness. I hire the surgeon to do a task.

Healthy marriages are all about a being with someone, not doing something to someone. All spouses need to feel heard, loved, accepted, and forgiven. This happens through the lens of relationships and being, and not through the lens of doing. I may hire a contractor to fix a plumbing problem. But I can't ask of my spouse to fix my mother or our child, let alone fix me. All spouses need to be responsible for themselves, and each spouse needs to be him or herself. When we ask our spouse to be responsible for us, we are placing a high ideal expectation that they never signed up for. I don't want my surgeon to say to me that the surgery do not go well because he was in a bad mood that day. But I do want my spouse to share

163

Do You Want To Pursue Ideal Expectations Or Do You Want To Pursue Realistic Expectations?

with me that they are hurting and had a bad day, so I can relate and be empathetic to them recognizing we all have bad days.

For example, let's say Peter is married to Kim. Kim comes to Peter complaining about her mom Martha. Kim's mom spoke to her in a critical, mean way. If Kim has ideal expectations, she will expect Peter to do something about what Martha has done or to somehow make Kim feel better. Kim has ideal expectations that Peter will call Martha and fix her by asking her to speak more respectfully to her daughter. Or Kim may ask Peter to drop everything he is doing and take her to her favorite ice cream shop to buy a milkshake. Now Kim is ideally expecting Peter to do something that is not his responsibility.

Expectations become confusing and frustrating for spouses when they are told to do something they never signed up to do. Kim's mom has been giving Kim troubles for many years, and when Kim feels dismissed or minimized by her mom, she also feels rejected. Kim is expecting Peter to take care of not only this issue, rejection, but also to take care of Kim and her hurt feelings by rearranging his schedule to take her to the ice cream store. It is one thing for Kim to share her feelings with Peter, and for Peter, out of kindness, to take her to the store. But if Peter is expected to do this out of fear, due to pressure from Kim, he now feels obligated and is no longer acting out of love.

Spouses with ideal expectations tend to want perfection. They tend to want their ducks lined up in a row and seek ways for life to go their way, as they have rules and ideas about how life should be. In addition, ideal expectations have to do with control. It is one thing to be in control of a task, for example, keeping the garage clean or to try to be in control of the service you receive from your plumber, but it is another thing to demand your spouse, the love of your life, to also stay under your control. When spouses expect their spouse to be perfect and not fail them or make a mistake, they are setting their spouse up to a high standard they never signed up for. The reality of life is when two spouses can be vulnerable, transparent and honest, this is when two people are wanting love and intimacy by confessing their brokenness and failures one to another.

One challenge for spouses who have idealistic expectations is not to compare their spouse to another spouse. It can be tempting to compare your spouse to someone else. You may say something like, "I wish my husband was as attentive to our children as that husband is." Or, "I wish my wife could learn to cook like Mary." Comparing your spouse to someone else leads to dissatisfaction and jealousy. So let's say Stacy and Nick are married, and Stacy says to Nick, "How come you don't do things for me like my friend Allison's husband Stan does for her? Allison brags about Stan at work, and all I hear is what Stan does. I'm thinking that I got short-changed, and I want our marriage to be like Allison and Stan. You need to go have a cup of coffee with Stan so you could learn how to be a better husband."

165

Do You Want To Pursue Ideal Expectations Or Do You Want To Pursue Realistic Expectations?

Imagine what it is like to be like Nick. He may start to think he needs to change and his wife may feel he needs to step it up and be like Stan. Nick may start to feel like a failure due to Stacy's critical words. Nick will feel the pressure to not be himself and try to be someone else to please Stacy, given he fears Stacy will continue to be unhappy and critical of him. His motivation to please and live up to these ideal expectations is based upon fear and not desire. It is almost like he feels Stacy is holding a gun to his head or watching his every move, scrutinizing how he treats her in comparison to how Stan treats Allison.

Unfortunately, far too often idealistic spouses can start to have romantic or emotional text, e-mail, or Facebook affairs with someone who appears to fit their ideal standards, as they become bored or disillusioned with their spouse and have a secret wish to be with someone ideal. They get together with their friends and vent about how their spouse has failed them or not lived up to some ideal expectation. Their friends also can join them in these complaints and may talk about their marriages and how unhappy they also are. Criticizing and complaining about your spouse to your friends or coworkers is not a good idea, as they will often validate how you feel or suggest you should pull away from your spouse, justifying your actions based upon how he or she is disappointing you. Friends may encourage ideal spouses that the grass is greener on the other side.

When one spouse has ideal expectations, the other spouse feels pressure to make them happy, to do things right, not to make mistakes or fail. When we ask our spouses not to fail us, we are asking them to fill a need inside of us in order for our world and marriage to be perfect. An idealist may have polarized views of good and bad wherein anything less than perfect is bad. People who feel this way often feel shame and put shame on others. This creates no win situation. Both spouses now are walking on eggshells feel bad and fearful of being declared a failure.

We all have experienced the challenge of pursuing excellence and the feelings of failure of not living up to excellence. We can be hard on ourselves, and we can't accept within ourselves the reality that we make mistakes as we keep undoing what we have accomplished, trying to get it right or perfect. This is bad enough for an individual, but also can affect our spouse and the health of our marriage. When one spouse is feeling and experiencing a low self-esteem due to not being perfect, this can affect the marriage. The marriage also suffers when we expect our spouses to be ideal and demand of them to become a perfect parent, perfect lover, have perfect health or perfect in the area of finances.

Consider the marriage of Tim and Lilly. Once they married, it did not take long for Tim to recognize that Lilly was a perfectionist. Although he had seen traits of this in their dating time, he was not ready for how idealistic Lilly was when then got married.

167

Do You Want To Pursue Ideal Expectations Or Do You Want To Pursue Realistic Expectations?

Lilly was obsessed with neatness. When Tim was in the living room, he reported it was like being in a museum where all the furniture had to be in place, no dirt allowed, and in reality, the living room was not for living but only for the guests they had over for dinner. Even the television room had to be kept in perfect order, and he was not allowed to put a cup down. Everything in the house had to be in place. Tim attempted to reason with Lilly, and sometimes they had arguments regarding the need for things to be perfect and Tim feeling criticized. He even complained that their love making had to be ideal based upon what he needed to do to prepare for any sort of intimacy or closeness. Meanwhile, Lilly saw Tim's failures as a sign that he didn't love her.

In cases like this, a battle starts to happen between the spouses. The challenge for the spouse with high expectations is this, how do you live with yourself, and how do you live with your spouse who is not ideal?

Healthy Intention: Focus on Realistic Expectations

As we all know, life is not perfect, people are not perfect, mistakes do happen, and the spouse you made a commitment to is going to let you down, intentionally or not, and hurt you. When spouses have realistic expectations, they make sure the marriage is more important than placing pressure on each other to grow or meet goals. They accept, like, and love each other just the way they are and do not ask each other to change or grow according to ideal desires. Individuals with realistic expectations make sure there is no fear or stubbornness in the relationship, and they desire to be kind to the other person, accepting them just the way they are. Acceptance and kindness come first; goals and expectations come second.

When spouses are ready to shift from demanding an ideal marriage to accepting a realistic marriage, this is when stress and pressures decrease. Unhealthy marriages demand ideal spouses. Healthy marriages accept realistic spouses. So when you decide to make the shift from demanding ideal expectations to pursuing realistic expectations, this means you do want to pursue and participate in a healthy marriage.

I am all for influencing each other when it comes to expressing some ideas or suggestions a husband or wife would ask their spouse to consider. Spouses do want each other to be happy or content. They do want to fulfill their spouse's occasional wants. But if a spouse moves from influence to demands and makes their spouse feel they need to change, then this will create an unhealthy marriage with unhealthy pressure on one or both spouses to be someone they are not. For example, I am all for two spouses to attend some workshop on parenting or attend some seminar of how they can manage their money better. But when one spouse demands or expects their spouse to attend these presentations and the one spouse does not want to, then it

169

Do You Want To Pursue Ideal Expectations Or Do You Want To Pursue Realistic Expectations?

is healthy to let it go and for the one spouse to go alone. I realize it is lonely to go alone, but you can't demand or put pressure on your spouse to participate. He or she must choose to do this, not feel pressured that they have to do something.

You see, realistic spouses realize that life is a journey, and when they get married, both people in a realistic way know they are going to rub off on each other and are going to want to change, evolve, and grow as the years go by. Helping one another grow and be their best is healthy. Asking your spouse to take ballroom dance lessons with you may be a good idea if both spouses are buying into this plan. Asking your spouse to go with you and take a six-week Italian cooking class at the local college also might be a good idea given both spouses are engaged and wanting to cook together in the kitchen to make delicious pasta dishes together. Spouses can change and grow based upon both spouses having realistic expectations regarding something they want to improve upon or add to their marriage.

It is okay to live in reality by coming up with some creative ideas for the marriage and for how the two of you could do something together. Growth and change happen over time as new ideas and opportunities present themselves. Ten years ago, there were no smartphones or tablets. Realistic spouses may both want to use these devices for the sake of living in the reality of how these devices can help their lives run more smoothly. However, it is unhealthy to place demands and wishes on a spouse to "be like the Joneses" and keep up with everyone else; if they fall behind and do not have the latest car, device, or activity for their kids, they start to feel they are failing and not living up to the idealistic expectations.

Marriage Struggles with Idealistic Expectations: What to Do

The cure or hope for the marriage to resolve this battle between the ideal versus the real is to grieve the loss of the ideal. To mourn is to put the necessary end to your wish for the ideal. It is to grieve the reality that your spouse is not going to be perfect, join you at all times in wanting to improve the marriage at your pace, and recognize he or she is just a human being. Putting endings and closure to the concept of ideal spouse and the ideal life is very important to living in reality, the reality of who your spouse really is.

This means you really wrap your head around the reality of accepting your spouse right now just the way they are. It is letting go of what the other person does not have and realistically viewing and accepting the person as they are. We all need to let go of what we don't get or let go of what we all wish, and live in reality of who we all really are. Ideal spouses expect you to make them happy; realistic people know you will let them down and that you are not expected to make them happy all the time.

Realistic expectations do value growth, and they accept the growth path each person is on. I do believe that life can be an arena for school and leaning, and when we are learning, we are growing.

171

Do You Want To Pursue Ideal Expectations Or Do You Want To Pursue Realistic Expectations?

This does not mean you always have to be growing or pushing yourself to keep on growing. It does not mean that you can't watch your favorite television shows or relax with a good book or movie (in fact, learning to relax and enjoy life could be considered an area of growth). If you have ideal expectations, you may feel that time is wasted when you are not using it to grow and push yourself to constantly be learning.

For example, on a Saturday morning if you can go to your favorite hardware store and take a class on various ways to paint a house, you feel you are growing. You may also ask your spouse to go with you to learn together. But if your spouse says no, this does not mean he or she is failing you. It is unhealthy to expect your growth is dependent on your spouse's growth. You want to grow together as a couple, which is good, but you may expect your spouse to grow at your pace and learn just like you, which can be damaging for the marriage.

So try saying to your spouse, "I want both of us to grow, but I am not going to demand that the way you want to grow matches the way I want to grow. I do want us to be growing and not become complacent with each other or with life. So from now on, I will do my best to accept you and not place demands on you to grow and change at my pace and learn to accept your ways and your pace. From now on, I may propose certain ideas or classes we could take, but if you choose not to go, I will not personalize this as you not wanting to be with me."

Complacency can happen to anyone when we fall into the temptation of being lazy, not trying, concluding this is the best it is going to be, and in general not wanting to participate in learning and growing. When two people are working together to help each other grow, the relationship can become healthy and realistic. In other words, there is a time and season for growth and change and there is a time for rest and relaxation.

Marriage Struggles with Realistic Expectations: What to Do

Probably the best way to live and grow with realistic expectations is to sit down with your spouse and ask each other: "What are your goals this year?" Healthy goal setting can help each spouse think of some goals they want for themselves and for the marriage. Each spouse could sit down and write out some personal goals and some marriage goals. These goals must be set in reality and not be ideal. So one spouse may say they want to lose ten pounds in the next year, or start a new hobby, or take an online class to help their skills for work, or maybe focus on a house project they would like to start doing. Goal setting can include how the two of you could be doing something together to grow and participate in a healthy marriage.

For example, maybe the two of you feel you need more fun in your life, so you plan once a month to go to the local concert hall and watch a live performance. Or maybe both spouses want to lose weight and be in better shape, so they have

173

Do You Want To Pursue Ideal Expectations Or Do You Want To Pursue Realistic Expectations?

a goal to go hiking three times a week and reduce their carbohydrate intake. As long as these goals are realistic and not demanding someone to be perfect but both people are on the journey towards growth, the two people are participating in a healthy marriage.

It really is okay to ask each other to participate in realistic expectations, as long as there is enough acceptance and kindness along the way. So if one spouse sets goals in a realistic way, this person needs to know that the other person is going to encourage them and observe them through the lens of acceptance and kindness. The last thing anyone wants to hear is their spouse criticizing and not accepting their pace and their way of growing. Each person needs to feel that the other person is their biggest cheerleader and is accepting how they are doing, expressing kindness and acceptance.

Ideal expectations say this: "I expect you to never be late for me, to always keep the house clean and perfect according to my standards. I also expect you to be highly responsible, never go into debt, pay your bills on time, and always be learning at a pace that matches my standards." Realistic expectations say this: "I accept you as my spouse, and I want us to encourage one another and not judge or control one another in how we grow. I know we are going to be late sometimes, we are going to make some mistakes and occasionally feel like not cleaning the house, and I know we sometimes will get into trouble with how we manage our money and may spend more than we make.

But that is okay, I do accept you."

So find a way to sit down with your spouse and make sure in the marriage that in all you do, both spouses know and feel they are loved, accepted, and there is kindness on board when each person makes a mistake. Lay down this realistic expectation foundation first before you go into conversations about growth and change. When one person starts to feel the tension and fear that they are not accepted and they start to notice in their spouse emotional reactions, criticism, or judging, the two spouses need to stop and converse about what is going on between the two of them. Fight for reality and pursue acceptance first so that both of you know you are invested in your marriage, and you love and like each other just as you are. Then you can enter into those conversations about goals and realistic expectations so that each spouse is walking in freedom, not fear, or stubbornness or feeling pressured. When both spouses each week sit down and hold each other accountable, they are living in reality, and they are living in kindness and acceptance. Be open to learn, grow, and change, but realize learning something new will take time, and view time as your friend so both spouses are choosing to be free.

CHAPTER 12
DIFFERENCE #10

DO YOU WANT TO PURSUE CONTROL
OR DO YOU WANT TO PURSUE FREEDOM?

Pre-chapter Quiz: Answer each statement either true or false as it pertains to you.

1. To avoid being alone, I tend to put up with someone who mistreats me.

2. In our marriage, I often feel alone and afraid, not having a voice.

3. I feel that my spouse thinks they can control everything about my life.

4. I feel that my spouse intentionally tries to intimidate me.

5. I feel jealous when I am not the first priority in our marriage.

6. I fear saying "no," as my spouse does not respect nor listen to my "no."

7. Despite the ways my spouse tries to control, I still seek to be free to be myself.

8. I wish my spouse and I could agree to disagree and stop controlling one another.

The goal of this last section is to help you understand the difference between controlling your spouse versus giving the gift of freedom as a way for your spouse and the marriage to feel free. Far too often, marriage becomes an arena in which spouses view their roles as a means to control one another. Even the line, "You are my spouse," can be used as a rationale to control one another with the conclusion, "You are mine." This results in the other spouse feeling they can't be themselves due to feeling controlled. But spouses who pursue freedom really want to accept and give the gift of freedom so each spouse knows they are free to be themselves. Control says obey. Freedom says accept.

UNHEALTHY INTENTION: FOCUS ON CONTROL

During your lifetime, someone other than your spouse has probably attempted to control you. We cannot altogether avoid people who crave control. Some people are more sensitive to control than others. Controlling people are all around us in different arenas such as work, school, church, friends, and family. If you grew up with a parent who was controlling, the last thing you want to do is to duplicate your family of origin by choosing a spouse who is controlling.

Spouses who pursue control do this in many different ways. They can be very aggressive or very passive or both: passive aggressive. They may

177

Do You Want to Pursue Control Or Do You Want to Pursue Freedom?

display this in their attitude, reactions, choices, and behaviors. People may display control in their use of time, various activities around the house, the way they converse, or in how they parent or manage money.

At its worst, pursuing control can bring about physical, emotional, verbal, or abusive patterns in the marriage. A spouse who may not have appeared controlling when you initially married may have a dark side that you did not know about. As the months or years go by, you start to feel or notice a pattern of control. Souses who have been married for 5 to 10 years look back, and they can say they noticed this person was controlling, but they just put up with it or thought they could change that person. Unfortunately, as you probably have experienced, trying to control or change a controlling spouse is crazy making and cannot be done. It is also false thinking to imagine your spouse will change due to YOUR efforts to control THEM. This only sets up a battlefield between two spouses trying to control using physical power or words of manipulation, and threat. This leads to a very unhappy marriage.

In general, spouses who pursue control are people who really do believe their way is the right way. Their motto is this: "Life has to go my way, and I will do life my way." Spouses who pursue control really are convinced others should be dependent upon them, and they want to guide others into doing life their way. If they can get you to depend on them and their way, then they feel life is going well.

In many ways, controlling people can be like kings who want to set up their kingdoms. Controlling people want to be the boss, the king and CEO of their company. Their goal is to build their kingdom, and they really do believe others should be their servants, obey them, and follow them. Their thinking is that they know what they are building, and they know best as the boss; therefore, others should follow and obey them. Controlling people really do like you to need them and depend upon them. Not that they will take care of you and provide for you, but the price you pay is submission. The followers of this leader cannot be independent or self-sufficient, as that would be a threat to the controller.

In addition, spouses who like to control also set up all the rules. If you live with a controlling spouse, you know the rules, you know your role, and you know your limits in what you can or cannot say. Understanding the rules and roles only leads to making sure you walk on eggshells so that you don't upset your spouse, and you constantly monitor your behavior to make sure you do not get out of line, as the consequences of doing this are not worth it. Upsetting or experiencing an angry, raging controller is painful. It is better to keep the peace, please him or her, and find a way not to allow yourself to pursue what you want or desire. All of us know what it feels like to experience someone judging us and demanding us to not upset his or her authority.

In addition, as you participate in this type of marriage, you also may experience your spouse

179

Do You Want to Pursue Control Or Do You Want to Pursue Freedom?

disliking the rules and laws in society. Those who want to control are often very comfortable in questioning or even outright looking for ways to disobey how as a society we are to function when it comes to laws. Take driving for example. Controllers disagree with the driving laws, thinking their speed or driving method is above the law. Someone stuck in controlling behavior really do believe they can get away with doing things their way and will test the limits of society. They will tell themselves that they don't have to obey or listen to others, as they feel their way is right.

When it comes to participating in a marriage, you had better make sure that you find a way to comply with a controlling strategy. It is not unusual for a compliant pleaser to marry a controller. A pleaser does not know how to say 'no' and a controller does not know how to hear a 'no.' Thus a pleaser is careful when to say 'no' as they have many memories of their controlling spouse reacting by going in to an angry rage. If you please a controller, he or she wins as they like people to affirm their stance. Unfortunately, the drive behind controlling behavior is the fear and anxiety of being controlled. So saying "no" to a controller becomes a tug-of-war, with the controller trying to get the upper hand to control you before they think you have an opening to control them. Their motto is this: No one is going to control me, so I had better be the boss and king and build my kingdom so no one threatens me. They are threatened if someone tries to control them, disagree with them and they feel threatened if you chose to have your own interests, without their approval, away from them.

The consequence of being married to someone who pursues this controlling stance is that you feel anxious and fearful, due to life having to go their way. Controllers will influence you to not question them, as they think they are right, and they will also manipulate you to feel that they never do anything wrong and you are to blame. Someone who is controlling may not realize how their ways hurt or affect others, or they may lack remorse or the desire to apologize, justifying hurts by believing they were deserved. Controllers tend to place blame, and they may feel shocked if someone else were to give them feedback that perhaps they also contributed to a particular problem.

Can a controlling spouse change? It happens slowly and in degrees maybe knocking down their level of control from a demanding ten to a negotiable six. If a controller can reduce their level of insistence and understand that they don't always have to be in control of others, maybe they can learn to release their need for life to always go their way. The challenge for a controller is to be reminded that they can be in control of themselves, but they have to find a way to negotiate with others, letting others also be in control of their lives. When a controller understands boundaries and that controlling others is not their duty, maybe they can control what they want, hear a "no," and accept someone else wanting their freedom without

181

Do You Want to Pursue Control Or Do You Want to Pursue Freedom?

that being a threat or insecurity for them. But until then, proceed with caution if you are relating to someone with controlling tendencies.

HEALTHY INTENTION: FOCUS ON FREEDOM

For a marriage to be free, each spouse needs to establish at the start of their marriage that each spouse is free. All spouses need to be responsible to be free to love, to choose, to express desires, to have their own thoughts, and to be free in their behavior how they act, spend time, money, and resources. To be free means you don't feel the pressure and demands to live according to someone else, but instead feel free to choose what you want and need for your own life.

So the challenge for your marriage is this: Is control so important to you that you are willing to let it hurt your marriage? Do you want to work with your spouse for the sake of building a trusting "we" marriage in which there is little to no control but instead each spouse practices self-control? All spouses need to have self-control over their lives and freedom. Each spouse needs to discern how "we" decisions are being made from a place of freedom and not from a place of control, in which one feels entitled or demands to do whatever they want. Even though we have freedom, we need to set limits on our own freedom.

Think of it this way. Let's say you have a credit card with a $5,000.00 limit. You are free to spend it any way you want and anywhere you want. You could just go to your favorite store, go on a shopping spree, choose the items you want, and charge them all on your credit card for the sake of taking home these items that day for your enjoyment.

But when the bill comes next month, do you have $5,000.00 to pay off this card? If you don't, you will go into debt. The credit card company will then charge you 12-17% each month on the outstanding balance if you only make the minimum payment. Sure, you have the card, you have the freedom, and you have the items you purchased. Just because you have the freedom does not mean you should use that freedom. In the same way, if you are given a driver's license, driving is a privilege, and you still have to obey all the many rules of the road because while you are free to drive, there are very serious consequences for driving too fast, recklessly, or under the influence of substances. All freedom must have limits.

In the same way, when it comes to our marriage, we all need limits, which is why we all need to have self-control with our freedom. So if your spouse asks you not to watch pornography on the internet because it hurts them, you will need to have self-control and set limits on watching porn due to the fact that your actions hurt your spouse and your marriage. Your spouse cannot control you, fix you, or stop you from watching porn. If they try, it creates co-dependency, which is not healthy.

183

Do You Want to Pursue Control Or Do You Want to Pursue Freedom?

The challenge in marriage relationships is to have conversations regarding control, self-control and freedom. One of the best ways to love and build healthy relationships is to think of ways to create and build freedom in the relationship for the sake of wanting to value freedom and not practice or pursue control. Each person needs to have the freedom to make their own choices when it comes to what items from a restaurant menu they want, or type of exercise or hobby they prefer to enjoy. Each person needs to be free, and allowed to make their own choices.

To be free means each person need to take ownership of their lives and their choices. For example, I need to feel free to take responsibility for my physical health. I need to find for myself what exercise program I like to do, what foods I should eat, and what foods I should avoid. I don't want my spouse to tell me what to do or how I should be eating or exercising. I need to have the freedom to take care of my health without someone else telling me how I should be eating or exercising.

The same can be true when it comes to other areas of my life: my feelings, thoughts, behaviors, and abilities. I need to have the freedom and the self-control to have my own feelings, know my thoughts and beliefs, and be in charge of my behavior, how I spend my time and money, where I work, and so forth.

You see, when there is freedom, there is love. Love says to each person, "You are free to be you, and I am free to be me." Love is a choice based upon my freedom to choose what or how I want to love, not according to your rules or your control. When two people are free, they can love from a place in which each has self-control. For example, because I love my wife and consider her, out of freedom, I want to be physically healthy for myself and for her. When I take ownership of my financial world in finding the freedom to have self-control and not go into debt, I am choosing out of love to find a way to be in control of my money and not ask another to be responsible for my debt.

Marriage Struggles with Control: What to Do

Up to this point, I have attempted to unpack the damage a controlling spouse can have on the marriage. When one spouse feels controlled, then they walk in fear and anxiousness cautious to take risks or disagree with their controlling spouse. But remember, the goal is to be free.

So how do we participate and practice freedom and self-control if you are in a controlling marriage? One of the best ways to really participate in freedom is to know what is yours. When you know what belongs to you, then you can take ownership of what is yours. For example, your feelings, thoughts, ideas, choices and desires are yours. It would be wise to sit down and take inventory of what belongs to you.

After you have discerned what is yours, then you can go into protection mode to set limits or boundaries of what belongs to you. Your goal is not to control your spouse but instead you want

185

Do You Want to Pursue Control Or Do You Want to Pursue Freedom?

to protect that which belongs to you. For example, if you buy a car with your money, you will want to protect it with locks and a car siren. You value your car and therefore you want to protect that which is yours. No one wants to allow someone to steal their car.

So in your marriage, attempt to communicate with your spouse by making up a list of what each spouse needs to take ownership and value, recognizing what belongs to them. It would be good for you to say things such as these are my feelings, these are my thoughts and ideas, and these are my choices and behaviors. Find a way to communicate what you know belongs to you by saying this is mine and that is yours. As each spouse takes ownership of what belongs to them then each spouse is taking ownership of what they value. Recognize that what you value in life is what should lead your heart and choices in life. This is not the time to play the blame game or finding fault with one another by trying to control the other person's values or choices.

Always remember this principle, you reap what you sow. If you sow to and cultivate what belongs to you, then you will reap the freedom of saying this is mine and participate in what is yours. Obviously, your controlling spouse does not like for you to have choices and walk in freedom. So the challenge is to communicate to your controlling spouse your choices and freedom is not being used as a strategy to get back at your spouse. They may protest and not like what is yours but as long as you communicate your intention is self-control and not spouse control, than maybe the two of you will be able to allow freedom to happen in your marriage.

Marriage Struggles with Freedom: What to Do

To participate in a marriage that really does value freedom and not control, each spouse needs to communicate each person free. To be free means you both can say both "yes" and "no" to the person you are relating to. It also means you can accept someone saying "yes" or "no" to you without getting angry and trying to fix or control. So if your spouse wants to drink a twelve-pack of beer each day, that person has the freedom to do this. You can't stop your spouse by telling them, "No, you can't do this." To set limits on someone by telling them what they can or cannot do is control. You can only set limits on what belongs to you based upon your freedom. You cannot use your freedom to try to force your spouse to stop drinking and change him or her. That does not work. But you can use your freedom to talk about how you feel and how you are affected and experience someone who drinks a twelve-pack of beer each day. You can also use your freedom to share with your spouse when they disrespect the budget and impulsively buy an item the two of you did not agree on buying. Communicating your feelings is being free; ordering your spouse to stop doing something you don't want them to do is controlling.

In your freedom, you can set limits. You could say to your spouse, "If you choose to drink, I will leave the house and take the children with me to the mall." Now your spouse is in control of the

187

DO YOU WANT TO PURSUE CONTROL OR DO YOU WANT TO PURSUE FREEDOM?

freedom to drink, and you are in control of your peace of mind and safety. Each person is acting out of freedom and not control. Out of freedom, you could find a way to have a conversation with your spouse in which you could say to him or her, "Can we both talk about this so we both can decide together whether drinking a twelve-pack of beer a day is something we want for this marriage?"

By having this conversation, you are in charge and free to share your feelings desires, and wants as an attempt to fight for freedom and build a healthier relationship. Maybe the two of you could see that drinking a couple of beers a day is okay, but not a twelve-pack. Somehow each person must take ownership and find the freedom to make their own choices without a hint of trying to control one another. The goal is for all of us to be free and for all of us to have self-control, not other-control, so that we all are choosing how we want to live our lives. In our freedom, we must all acknowledge our own conscience—look at ourselves in the mirror to decide what we truly value and want to do. I am free to steal from my employer and watch porn, but I also must face the consequences for myself if I get caught (or even if I don't), and how this affects me, my spouse and our marriage. Watching porn or stealing from my boss may make me feel better, and I am acting out of freedom, but I still need to face the consequences of my actions.

So sit down with your spouse and ask these questions: "Is there room in this relationship to talk about freedom and discern what you are free to do, what I am free to do, and for the two of us, how we cultivate freedom in this marriage? Can we be sensitive to make sure we try not to control one another, or selfishly use our freedom to do whatever we want to do? Can we hold each other accountable so that if I engage in an activity that hurts you, we both can share our hurts so we both value the other and don't intentionally hurt each other in our freedom?"

Imagine what a healthy marriage would look like when spouses stop controlling one another and instead they value freedom so that each person had self-control. When two spouses are free, there is room to negotiate, to discuss matters, and to find a place where both people feel like they are winning. When control is happens, both are losing, and there is no freedom, as each spouse tries to please the other and is walking in fear and not freedom. But when control and fear leave the marriage, then both spouses feel the freedom to be responsible for their choices, and there is a lifetime of choosing to be free.

So fight for freedom and not control. Have conversations which emphasize freedom and self-control. Your marriage will be healthy as each spouse stops accusing each other and starts accepting each other. When you accuse, you are controlling. When you accept, you are valuing freedom. Be free, don't control others and don't let someone control you. Set limits on how much time you want to spend with someone who is controlling. You were created to be free, free to be you, free to make your

189

Do You Want to Pursue Control Or Do You Want to Pursue Freedom?

own choices, and free to pursue your own desires. Take ownership over what belongs to you.

PART THREE

KEYS TO IMPROVE YOUR MARRIAGE

CHAPTER 13

KEYS TO IMPROVE YOUR MARRIAGE

My goal in part three is to provide hope and solutions for each spouse and for both spouses on how they can make some improvements for the marriage. My goal is for each spouse to assess which unhealthy intentions you identify with and what steps you can take to change them. If you are married to someone with unhealthy intentions, what are some steps you can take to approach your spouse for the purpose of working with him or her so both of you are participating in building a healthy marriage? Remember this, it takes two to reconcile and work together, but it only takes one to decide to do something different and make changes for the marriage. Far too often, spouses will not change because they are waiting for their spouse to make the first move. But as the title of this book suggests, I want you to participate and build a healthy marriage, as you learn the differences between unhealthy intentions and healthy intentions. Be a difference maker.

Healthy marriages are not about studying the other spouse, trying to figure them out, and looking at what they do wrong, according to you. Instead, take the first step and make the first move toward building a healthy marriage. It is easy to look through the window and observe your spouse. But change happens when each spouse looks in the mirror and assesses how they are functioning and decides to focus on what they can do.

9781530200238

take the first step and make the first move toward building a healthy marriage. It is easy to look through the window and observe your spouse. But change happens when each spouse looks in the mirror and assesses how they are functioning and decides to focus on what they can do.

take the first step and make the first move toward building a healthy marriage. It is easy to look through the window and observe your spouse. But change happens when each spouse looks in the mirror and assesses how they are functioning and decides to focus on what they can do.

CHAPTER 14

KEYS FOR EACH SPOUSE

BEGIN WITH EXAMINING YOURSELF

The goal is for you to assess each of these 10 differences and say to yourself: "My bad, I recognize I do that." Start with you and decide what you can do to change. Remember the goal is for you to do an accurate and honest feedback of yourself. Search and know yourself and consider what areas you do need to make improvements. Come out of denial and really live in the reality of who you really are. We are all broken and imperfect and none of us do these 10 healthy intentions perfectly. You know your flaws, your spouse knows your flaws, so take a look at yourself in the mirror and really began the process of making some changes to improve your marriage.

How do you do this? Take out a sheet of paper and go back over the 10 differences. At the top of the page write this title: Low Frequency. Go through each of the ten and under this low frequency title, write down which of the 10 unhealthy differences you do not do. A low frequency means you do not do or occasionally you recognize that you do this. Maybe you rated yourself a 2 when it comes to focusing on past hurts or present hurts. When you approach your spouse, you can recognize you do not focus on past hurts and resentments by bring them up all the time. That is good and it shows a level of maturity on your part to not focus on the past. Congratulate yourself for not bringing up the past when you and your spouse are resolving a conflict. Celebrate which of those ten unhealthy differences you wrote down as a low frequency.

OWN YOUR PAIN

Now that you have identified which of the top ten unhealthy differences you assigned a low frequency, next take out a second sheet and write down this Title: Occasional Frequency. Go through these 10 unhealthy differences and assign a number as a 5 or 6. This number 5 or 6 can be used as a rating to notice within these ten differences, there are some unhealthy patterns in which you occasionally do that does damage the marriage.

After you have listed maybe 3 or 4 of these 10 unhealthy differences under this title occasional frequency, answer this question: "How much does it bother me that I do these things?" Maybe you assigned a 5 in which the unhealthy difference is in demanding ideal expectations. Can you look at yourself in the mirror and realize once in a while you do engage in this unhealthy intention-placing demands on your spouse to live up to your high expectations. It may bother your spouse that you expect a lot from him or her, but does it bother you when you contribute to the pain and sadness between the two of you? Can you see yourself saying: "I don't like that part of me that demands high standards from my spouse, and this is something I am not too proud of?" When you can feel your own pain, this will hopefully motivate you to start changing and doing something about your pain. Allow pain to be your teacher. Use this pain to focus on you so that you take responsibility of this area and you do feel sad how you do place ideal expectations on your spouse. Does this really bother you, do you feel bad and sad, and can you see how the marriage is unhealthy due to this demand you ask of your spouse to be perfect? Examine yourself and ask this question: "Why do I expect my spouse to be perfect? What stress and fear is going on in our marriage that results in me watching him or her and in my reaction, I place undue pressure on my spouse? What is it about me where I try and I try to reduce any mistake in our marriage so that we are always pushing ourselves to have a marriage with little to no mistakes? I wonder how this affects my spouse and our kids."

ACCOUNTABILITY PARTNERS

The third step is to take out another sheet of paper and write at the top this title: High Frequency. On this sheet, go through the 10 unhealthy differences and assign a rating number of 7-9 stating this is a high frequency you know you do on a regular basis and it is ruining your marriage. You can assess yourself and you can understand how unhealthy it is to engage in these unhealthy behaviors. Usually these high frequency unhealthy differences come from a place of reacting. Examine yourself and ask: "Why do I react so quickly? How do I feel about how I react? Is my reaction working and bringing about the desired results I was looking for? Are my unhealthy reactions resulting in a close relationship, and are they building trust in this marriage?" Spouses who participate in reacting rather than responding unfortunately sow unhealthy patterns. When you react, you are coming from a place of anxiousness or fear. To react is to focus on the other person. To respond is to focus on you. Responders slow down the pace and tone of the conversation by pausing to listen to the other person, not just hear words or accusations. When you react, you are accusing. When you respond, you are accepting.

On this sheet of high frequency, maybe you did assign an 8 in your unhealthy intention to want to correct. Can you look at yourself in the mirror and recognize how trying to react by correcting your spouse all the time is hurting the marriage and it is hurting you? Your spouse is either defensive, reacts and argues back or he or she has shut down and is quiet. Your need to correct is not only hurting your spouse but also is it hurting you. Does this pain of trying to correct bring about some pain and sorrow for you due to your high frequency of trying to judge and correct your spouse all the time?

In addition, think of three close friends you can trust and be honest with. Contact all three of them and ask if you could meet for a cup of coffee. Bring this book and share with them a few unhealthy intentions you rated as high in your frequency of doing them. Make a copy of the sheet you titled 'High Frequency' of those unhealthy intentions that you assigned as a 7-9. Explain to them you are reading this book and give them each a sheet of those high frequency unhealthy differences you know you do on a regular basis. Tell your friends what you want to work on to change you, in order to become a better person and a better spouse. Become vulnerable by sharing what you have learned or noticed about yourself regarding those specific unhealthy intentions.

When you get together, ask them to be honest with you and this question: "In the time you have known me, have you experienced me correcting you, being selfish, or always having the need to be right? I sense I do this in my marriage, and I react and do this to my spouse, but have you also noticed this in our friendship?"

By doing this, you are asking for intentional feedback from your friends. You want to listen to them to see if they notice and experience these unhealthy intentions. As them to be honest with you as you are serious about this and you do want to make some changes for your marriage. Explain to them you have become more aware of yourself as a spouse by reading this book, but you also want to hear their feedback of how they experience you as a friend. Tell them not to sugar coat their answers and be prepared to listen and not react if they do see you as someone who is controlling, critical or always having to be right?

Remember, you cannot change yourself by yourself. It would be great if we could all just flip a switch and stop a behavior right away. But that is not how life works. So ask your friends and really listen to them without getting defensive if they also validate how they experience you. In addition, ask your friends to hold you accountable to working on yourself and these unhealthy intentions. Ask them to give you a phone call once a week or text you and ask how you are doing and how you have been treating your spouse this week. I know this means you have to be vulnerable and transparent by trusting them. But if you are serious about wanting to change some of these intentions, you need to be held accountable.

DECLARATION PAGE TO YOURSELF

Another solution is to make out a declaration page. Let me explain. Sit down in front of the computer and create this title: My Declaration Page of Promise and Vow to My Spouse. Then list three or four vows or promises that you will attempt to make for the sake of the marriage. Focus on those high frequency unhealthy intentions you wrote in this last exercise. For example, consider this format:

Promise # 1: *I promise to stop looking for ways to correct my spouse. I know this hurts you, hurts me, and hurts our marriage. I have asked three friends to hold me accountable to daily participate in stopping this hurtful intention. I also want to earn your trust by not just saying it but practicing it so that you can trust me to do my best and resist the urge to try to correct you. Instead of correcting, I want to practice saying words of acceptance.*

Type up three or four unhealthy intentions and how you want to stop these. Make three or four copies and tape them around the house. Put them on your mirror or on your refrigerator or any place that you look at daily so you see this list and remind yourself of your intention to stop doing this unhealthy intention. Daily remind yourself that you are taking this seriously and you do want to self-correct and change not only for you but for the sake of your marriage.

Also write down any consequences you want to give yourself if you fail to do these things. Maybe you could write you are not going to go to your favorite coffee house for a week, or maybe you are going to do something around the house that you have been procrastinating. Or maybe you will get out a jar and put money in it when you don't follow through. At the end of the month you can donate this to your favorite charity. The point is this: communicate to your spouse that you are serious and you do want to stop some of these unhealthy intentions.

If you did this, imagine how your spouse might react. Be prepared for a conversation in which your spouse will look at you crossed-eyed and confused as you explain how you want to change. Share that it is your desire to keep this marriage and that you want to change for the sake of creating a healthier marriage. Be vulnerable and honest, asking your spouse to be patient as you confess that you are exhausted from trying to accuse, blame, and correct your spouse, and instead you want to focus on changing yourself finding various ways to stop doing these unhealthy intentions. Explain you are serious and you want to stop these things and never go back to doing them again. Confess and repent to your spouse how sorry you do feel and it is your goal to become a better spouse for him or her. Remind your spouse to be patient as you began the process stopping these unhealthy patterns and never wanting to go back and do them again.

BE A TORTOISE AND NOT A HARE

Do you remember the tale of the tortoise and the hare? Remember the tortoise wins. Think of it this way. What if you were diagnosed with stage 3 cancer? How motivated would you be to get this cancer out of your body? Could you see it is going to take some time to do surgery, radiation, and chemotherapy? You are okay with this time frame because you are willing to be patient for the sake of getting this cancer out of your body. To get the bad and unhealthy intentions out means you have to be patient or think like a tortoise. We all want to do things quickly, as we live in a society that wants instant results. But value being a tortoise and take the slow path of wanting to change and stick to that plan. The tortoise wins, and my hope is you too can win by becoming a healthier spouse..

CHAPTER 15

KEYS FOR BOTH SPOUSES

If you find you are married to someone who displays some of these unhealthy intentions, I want you to find a way to enter into conflict resolution by involving your spouse in these key activates listed below for your marriage. I want you to consider the words of Benjamin Franklin to help you in working with your spouse who displays unhealthy intention:

"Tell me and I forget, teach me and I may remember, involve me and I will learn."

Telling your spouse to do this and not do that is not working. Your spouse will not listen, especially if you do it with a nagging, angry tone. You also must be careful not to take on a teaching role with your spouse. This creates a one-up one-down role that is unhealthy. Spouses get suspicious about why you are trying to teach them, as they may feel your goal is to control them to do something your way. The spouse receiving this teaching may feel belittled or put down, and this teaching approach may lead to your spouse intentionally not wanting to remember.

But if you can engage and participate with your spouse in the process of correcting unhealthy intentions, then you have a better chance of learning to grow for the sake of the marriage. Value being a team player working together to build a healthy marriage.

ADMIT WE HAVE A PROBLEM

As best you can, before the conversation heads into a sixty-minute fight, take your spouse's hand and invite him or her to sit down on the couch to discuss something that is weighing on your mind. Say to your spouse that you have made a mistake and you take ownership for this mistake. Say you know this mistake affects both of you as now you are alone, disconnected, blaming, and finding fault. Share that you both are being defensive of your positions. Share how you feel hurt, angry, and disconnected, and ask how he or she feels about how you fight when a problem comes up. Ask your spouse if we can both take ownership and responsibility regarding our part in contributing to the disconnection.

Admit We Both Feel Hurt

Next talk about the hurt you are feeling about how you two argue. Communicate and say you feel sad and hurt in how you two communicate anger and blame. Ask your spouse, "How do you feel about how we are arguing?" Explain to him or her you feel hurt, and empathize how your spouse probably also feels hurt. For example, maybe the hurt reflects disrespect. Can you say to your spouse, "I feel hurt because I feel disrespected, and I imagine in the way I talk to you, you also must feel disrespected? Is that what you are feeling?" The goal is to express how you both feel hurt and are affected by the way you are talking and treating each other. Share with your spouse that you do not want to blame or find fault anymore, as this only brings hurt to the marriage.

Admit the Effects on the Marriage

Third, talk about how these hurts are affecting not only you as an individual but the two of you as a couple in how you talk and treat each other. Say something like this: "When we fight like this, I feel sad because I hurt you, and instead of us loving one another, we are being mean to each other." Share and be vulnerable how these unhealthy intentions affect the marriage. For example, maybe you are sleeping in separate rooms, finding ways to avoid each other, and feeling tension being around each other. Share how you sense both of you tend to walk on eggshells around each other to avoid another fight. Take ownership and admit what you have done now and in the past, to contribute to being disconnected and feeling alone in your marriage. Be honest and confessing, not blaming and accusing. This will begin the process of building trust and emotional connection.

Share Your Desires

Share with your spouse what you want and what you desire for the two of you. Share with your spouse that your hope is for the two of you to find a new way to resolve conflict so that both of you can relate in a much healthier way. Say to your spouse: "What I really desire is that when a problem arises, we both respond and not react with unhealthy intentions which only lead to distance." Ask your spouse what they desire and want for the marriage. Discover and discern how the two of you can participate and learn what you desire for the sake of conflict resolution.

Share Your Needs

Share with your spouse what you need. Maybe you need words of reassurance that your spouse will be there for you. Or share your need for comfort and empathy. Your needs are very important, and it is important to tell your spouse what you need in the moment. Say to him or her, "Honey, what I need are words of kindness when a problem or mistake happens in our marriage. I have needs, and you have needs. Can we find a way to meet each other's needs and not just solve or identify the problem? I don't want us to keep doing what we have been doing, because I feel insecure and scared, as we both just don't like each other anymore, and this leads to the fear that you will leave me or not really care about how I feel. I need for you to listen to my needs, and I will listen to your needs. Maybe if we express what we need, we will find a way to meet each other's needs and enjoy each other rather than blaming each other." It is a beautiful thing to get into the habit of asking your spouse, "What do you need from me?"

Value Apologizing

When was the last time you apologized to your spouse for your part in what you contributed to a fight or argument? Do you find this uncomfortable, or do you resist because your pride gets in the way? To apologize means having to be humble and swallow your pride for the sake of confessing and admitting your part in what you did and how sorry you feel for contributing to mistrust, hurt, and pain. To apologize also means to show empathy and compassion to your spouse by really being sorry for bringing hurt and pain to your spouse. If you can take the lead and do this, then maybe your spouse can also learn to do this for the sake of the marriage, recognizing how the hurt or pain has now affected the marriage.

Apologizing may or may not heal the hurt; some hurt does take time to heal. But at the very least, if you can apologize, you can say with words and expression how sorry and compassionate you feel for bringing hurt to your spouse and to your marriage. Say to your spouse that you know just saying the words can help, but you also know that healing the hurt may take time, and you understand this process. This saying is not true: "Love means you never have to say you are sorry."

Preserve the Good

As best you can, find a way to hold onto what is good about your marriage. Even when you and your spouse are arguing, focus on how much you feel loved and how proud you are of all the two of you have done in the years together and share this with your spouse. The principle is this: Don't let any fight or argument sabotage the good you have going in the marriage. Count your blessings and be grateful for the areas in which you have a good marriage. Tell your spouse that despite this current conflict, deep down you do love and care for your spouse, and you do choose "us."

Practice Forgiveness

When you are ready, try to model and practice forgiveness. To forgive someone is to cancel the debt or mistake they made that hurt you and hurt the marriage. To forgive is to say to the person: "You don't owe me anything, and I am not going to hold onto this memory or this fight and use this hurt as a weapon to punish you later." When you are ready to forgive, you are not only doing this for the marriage, but you are also doing this for yourself. To forgive is to let go and not participate in holding onto resentments, grudges, and hostility. When two people find a way to forgive one another, they stop being stuck and find a way to move on. This does not mean you forget, and it does not mean you will get over the hurt right away. But at the very least, you do want to practice forgiving.

Pursue Reconciliation

To reconcile means both spouses can say what they have learned from an argument and what they are going to do differently next time as a way to keep building trust, closeness, and intimacy again. Seek and find ways to pursue trust, and as trust builds, both of you will feel more comfortable letting down your walls of self-protection. To reconcile is to return to the "we" and become close and emotionally connected again for the sake of desiring intimacy.

Learn How to Give

Look for ways to fight for your marriage, moving from hostile accusations to caring acceptance; learn to show acts of love, kindness, and care toward your spouse. Probably the best way to do this is not only to learn the ten differences explained in this book, but also to learn about giving. Let me unpack what I mean.

In general, there are three ways in which spouses express either hurt or love towards each other: taking, getting, and giving. Everyone expresses each of these attitudes at times, but if you constantly take or get, you will remain stuck in your unhealthy marriage. When we take, we make the marriage all about ourselves, find ways to criticize and control, and look for ways to bring up and hang on to resentment. What do I mean? When we take, we look at each conversation or encounter with our spouse and take what we believe belongs to us. Someone with a taking attitude views their spouse as theirs, giving themselves permission to control, criticize, correct, and demand ideal expectations.

A second attitude is getting. A lens of getting views each conversation or encounter as a means to get something. Each transaction is like a sales transaction in which someone gives in order to get something back. Givers give to get. For example, we may give love, acceptance, encouragement, or forgiveness, all the while looking for an exchange. It's easy to view giving as a condition: I give to you, you give to me. Getting something becomes the motive behind giving. Again, this is unhealthy and hurtful for your marriage. A healthy marriage does not look at each transaction with the intention of taking or getting, trying to manipulate or coerce your spouse to participate in the game of take and get. A marriage is not like a retail store in which I give my money in exchange to get an item. But that can't happen in your marriage.

So the final attitude of what breeds and feeds a healthy marriage is when two spouses choose and want to give. Spouses who give love, acceptance, encouragement, and mercy deeply desire to want to express love in the form of giving. Givers have in their hearts compassion, empathy, kindness and understanding which motivates them to want to give. They give these gifts of love with no strings attached just because they love you. Givers give favors the receiver may not deserve but do not feel obligated to give favors based upon some owing system. Givers give generously.

Look for ways to give, not to take or get. Takers look for ways to justify their accusations, getters look for ways for fairness wanting an even exchange, and givers give with no strings attached. Pursue and fight for being a giver and give healthy intentions generously. If you notice your spouse consistently taking or getting, find a way to discuss this, and if you can't, find a good therapist to work with you and your spouse to have conversations in which both spouses want to move from accusing each other to accepting one another. And I promise, as you do this, your marriage happiness and satisfaction will be till death do us part!

CHAPTER 16

SUMMARY

To summarize, I hope this book has challenged your way of behaving by revealing the top 10 unhealthy intentions for your marriage. And I hope when you identify those unhealthy intentions, you will look at yourself in the mirror and assess if this is working for you and your spouse. Can you see how unhealthy intentions damage a marriage and hurt both you and your spouse? Can you see how changing unhealthy intentions to healthy intentions will lead to a healthy marriage? Can you recognize doing unhealthy intentions will keep you stuck in accusations and how changing and participating in healthy intentions will lead to acceptance? Is that what you want?

The purpose of this book is to make your marriage better by moving from accusing one another to accepting one another. It is not easy to change given you may have been doing and engaging in some of these unhealthy intentions for years. Please don't give up and falsely conclude this is a good as it gets and assume, this is me and that is just the way it is. Start focusing by engaging in the healthy 10 differences first. As you do this, the unhealthy intentions will start to lesson in frequency as you really practice and participate in wanting to participate in the top 10 healthy intentions.

So catch your words early by pausing and reflecting before your react and find a way to apologize confessing you blew it and how sorrowful you do feel you did it again. Be reminded you are not perfect-nor is your spouse. Reassess why you married your spouse. You did marry for love and companionship so as to not be alone and join someone for the journey doing life together. Desire love, acceptance, and being together with your spouse building a better marriage. And I promise this: If you both are wanting to stop accusing each other and move to accepting each other, you will have a happy and healthy marriage.

NOTES

1. Chapter 5: Do You Want to Correct or Do You Want to Accept? Pg. 45: Billy Joel, "Just The Way You Are," by Billy Joel, in *The Stranger*, Columbia Records, 1997.

2. Chapter 6: Do You Want to Criticize or Do You Want to Encourage? Pg. 59: Kenny Rogers, "She Believes In Me," by Steve Gibbs, in *The Gambler*, United Artist, 1979.

3. Chapter 8: Do You Pursue Justice or Do You Want to Pursue Mercy? Pg. 76: Orianthi Panagaris, "According To You," by Orianthi Panagaris, in *Believe*, Geffen Records, 2009.

4. Pg. 80: Les Miserables, 2012. Directed by Tom Hooper, USA: Universal Pictures, 2012. Film.

5. Chapter 10: Do You Want to Focus on Past Hurts or Present Hurts? Pg. 102: Kenny Rogers, "Through The Years," by Steve Dorff & Marty Panzer, in *Share Your Love*, Liberty Records, 1982.

About the Author

Phillip Kiehl is a Licensed Marriage & Family Therapist and a Board Certified Chaplain. He maintains a private practice in the Los Angeles area providing services to individuals and marriages for over 20 years. In addition, he has worked in various psychiatric hospitals, counseling centers and drug and alcohol clinics for the last 30 years. He is a native of California and pursued his Masters in Psychology at California State University, Los Angeles and also pursed a Masters in Theology at Fuller Seminary in Pasadena, California.

Phillip, and his wife Cynthia, partner together to help people move from accusing one another to accepting one another. They love to help and encourage spouses to deepen their marriage relationship by recognizing the top ten difference between healthy and unhealthy patterns in the way they treat one another. They live in Southern California with their two dachshund dogs Reggie and Ruby.

Phillip loves to teach and speak providing couple's workshops and retreats motivating people to continue to make marriage work. You can contact him regarding any questions or for speaking engagements at **www.philkiehl.com** or at **phillipkiehl@gmail.com.**